WOMEN SEA

Global employment policies and practices

CW00690461

WOMEN SEAFARERS
Global employment policies and practices

International Labour Office
in collaboration with the
Seafarers International Research Centre

Contributing authors
P. Belcher, H. Sampson, M. Thomas, J. Veiga and
M. Zhao

INTERNATIONAL LABOUR OFFICE•GENEVA

ILO
Women seafarers: Global employment policies and practices
Geneva, International Labour Office, 2003

Woman worker, seafarer, employment, conditions of employment, working conditions, developed country, developing country. 14.04.2

ISBN 92-2-113491-1

ILO Cataloguing in Publication Data

The designations employed in ILO publications, which are in conformity with United Nations practice, and the presentation of material therein do not imply the expression of any opinion whatsoever on the part of the International Labour Office concerning the legal status of any country, area or territory or of its authorities, or concerning the delimitation of its frontiers.

The responsibility for opinions expressed in signed articles, studies and other contributions rests solely with their authors, and publication does not constitute an endorsement by the International Labour Office of the opinions expressed in them.

Reference to names of firms and commercial products and processes does not imply their endorsement by the International Labour Office, and any failure to mention a particular firm, commercial product or process is not a sign of disapproval.

ILO publications can be obtained through major booksellers or ILO local offices in many countries, or direct from ILO Publications, International Labour Office, CH-1211 Geneva 22, Switzerland. Catalogues or lists of new publications are available free of charge from the above address or by email: pubvente@ilo.org.

Visit our website: http://www.ilo/org/publns

Typeset by Magheross Graphics, France & Ireland, *www.magheross.com*
Printed and bound in Great Britain by Biddles Ltd, *www.biddles.co.uk*

PREFACE

In the past 50 years women have come to be employed in steadily increasing numbers aboard the world's merchant ships. Although their presence has occasionally attracted comment, the report presented here is the first comprehensive study of the policies and practices of the employment of women seafarers.

This study was commissioned by the International Labour Office (ILO) following the resolution concerning women seafarers adopted by the 29th Session of the Joint Maritime Commission on 22–26 January 2001 in Geneva. The research was conducted by the Seafarers International Research Centre (SIRC) at Cardiff University in the United Kingdom.

The SIRC research team received the cooperation of many women seafarers, trade unions, shipowners and ship managers as well as training and regulatory institutions in all world regions. I would like to thank them all for having taken the enquiry so seriously and for having participated so willingly. I believe this book will be of considerable benefit to the ever-growing numbers of women seafarers and to all those who are involved and interested in improving the conditions and welfare of women employed on board the world's merchant ships in the twenty-first century.

Cleopatra Doumbia-Henry
Acting Director
Sectoral Activities Department
International Labour Organization

CONTENTS

ACKNOWLEDGEMENTS

The SIRC research team engaged in this study was made up of Phillip Belcher, Dr. Helen Sampson, Dr. Michelle Thomas and Dr. Jaime Veiga, and was led by Dr. Minghua Zhao. Dr. Zhao was also responsible for shaping the manuscript into its final form. Part of the statistics on women's participation in the cruise sector cited from published sources was produced by Dr. Bin Wu and drawn from the SIRC's Global Seafarers Database; Prof. Tony Lane contributed to the editing of the first draft of the report; and Prof. Michael Bloor kindly lent a hand with the drafting of the section on methodology. Data for this study were gathered with the assistance of SIRC collaborators in several world regions, including: Dr. Doina Carp (Romania), Ruxing Cheng (China), Diana Factuar (Philippines), Vivek Jain (Singapore), Revd. Maria Jimenez (United States), Prof. Fancun Kong (China), Prof. Xavier Martinez and Dr. Ricardo Rodriguez-Martos (Spain), Revd. David Mesenbring (United States), Kathy Metcalf (United States), Dr. Kiki Mitroussi (Greece), Prof. Mats Rosendal (Sweden), Torsten Schroder (Germany), Jacqueline Smith (United States), Laila Svendsen (Sweden) and Capt. Willi Wittig (Germany). The research team received full clerical support from Maria Goldoni and Louise Deeley at the SIRC, Cardiff University. Finally, acknowledgement and grateful thanks must be extended to Charlotte Beauchamp (ILO) who provided tremendous encouragement and support throughout the editing process of this book, to Margareta Simons who carefully edited the manuscript, and to the many men and women who so generously gave their time to participate in the research and without whom the study would not have been possible.

TERMINOLOGY

Abbreviations

AMA	Antwerp Maritime Academy
BIMCO	Baltic and International Maritime Council
BTB	Belgian Transport Workers' Union
CAWU	Central Amalgamated Workers Union
CEEP	European Centre of Enterprises with Public Participation and of Enterprises of General Economic Interest
CIAGA	Centro de Instrução Almirante Graça Aranha
CMU	Constanza Maritime University
ENIDH	Escola Náutica Infante D. Henrique
ENMM	Ecole Nationale de la Marine Marchande de Marseille
ESIU	Estonian Seafarers International Union
ETUC	European Trade Union Confederation
EU	European Union
FETCM	Federación Estatal de Transportes, Comunicaciones y Mar (de la Unión General de Trabajadores)
FMST	Faculty for Maritime and Transport Studies
FNB	Facultad de Náutica de Barcelona (de la Universitat Politècnica de Catalunya)
GCBS	General Council of British Shipping
GCMS	Glasgow College of Maritime Studies
HESA	Higher Education Statistics Agency
HR	Human resources
ILO	International Labour Office/Organization
IMEC	International Maritime Employers' Committee

IMO	International Maritime Organization
IOMMP	International Organization of Masters, Mates and Pilots
ISF	International Shipping Federation
ISL	Institute of Shipping Economics and Logistics
ITF	International Transport Workers' Federation
ITUMF	Istanbul Technical University, Maritime Faculty
MARCOM	Maritime Communications
MCA	Maritime and Coastguard Agency
MET	Maritime education and training
NATFHE	National Association of Teachers in Further and Higher Education
NGO	Non-governmental organization
NMOA	Norwegian Maritime Officers Association
NMS	National Maritime Section (of the NSZZ Solidarność)
NSU	Norwegian Seamen's Union
NUMAST	National Union of Maritime and Aviation Shipping Transport Officers
NZOU	New Zealand Officers Union
OBE	Order of the British Empire
OECD	Organisation for Economic Co-operation and Development
PSU	Polish Seafarers Union
RMT	Rail and Maritime Transport Union
SEKO	Union for Service and Communication
SIMA	Svendbore International Maritime Academy
SINCOMAR	Sind. de Capitães e Oficiais da Marinha Mercante
SIRC	Seafarers International Research Centre
SMS	College of Applied Engineering and Maritime Studies
SMU	Shanghai Maritime University
SPA	Social Policy Agreement
STCW	Standards of Training, Certification and Watchkeeping
TUMM	Tokyo University of Mercantile Marine
UNICE	Union of Industrial and Employers' Confederations of Europe
WID	Women in Development
WMU	World Maritime University

Explanatory note

Certain terms and expressions relating to the structure of the shipping industry as well as to the hierarchy on board ship have been used in this report. For those unfamiliar with the shipping industry, this short note should shed some light on them.

The world's shipping industry comprises approximately 87,000 ships, with the purpose of offering a transportation or entertainment service to goods or people. It is more commonly known as merchant (in contrast to naval) shipping. Within merchant shipping, there are two distinct sectors: passenger shipping, which offers a holiday, entertainment and transportation service to people on board cruise ships and ferries; and cargo shipping, which provides a transportation service for raw materials and manufactured goods on board various types of cargo ships. Cargo ships are designated by the types of cargoes they carry, and so container ships carry containers, tankers carry liquids and bulk carriers carry raw materials such as iron ore or coal in bulk.

The person in charge of the vessel is the captain, who is also known by the legal term of the master or sometimes colloquially as "the Old Man". There are three main departments or sectors on cargo ships: deck, navigation and cargo; engineering; and catering. The departments are organized in a hierarchical manner, with various roles divided between the officers and the ratings. In passenger shipping, the ship is run in a similarly hierarchical manner under the command of the captain. However, because of the much larger number of people on board (typically, there are between 20 and 30 crew on a cargo vessel compared with several thousands of people on a cruise vessel), there is a greater need for departments dealing with the needs of the crew and passengers. Consequently, the deck and engineering departments (which are collectively termed the marine department/sector) are supplemented by departments dealing with the hotel side of the vessel, which include: entertainment; cruise; administration; housekeeping; and food and beverage. For a glossary of terms, see below:

Term	Explanation
AB	Able bodied, a senior rating in the deck department
Cadet	Trainee officer
Captain, Master, Old Man	The person in charge of the ship
Chief Engineer	Head of the engineering department
Chief Officer, the Mate	Head of the deck department

Flag out	The procedure undertaken when changing the registry of a ship from the country of domicile of the owner/operator to another, which is normally a flag of convenience country
Flag of convenience	A flag of a country under which a ship is registered in order to avoid financial charges or restrictive regulations in the owner's country
Marine department/sector	Collective term for the deck and engineering departments
Merchant navy	United Kingdom term for commercial shipping
Pilot	A locally engaged navigation expert employed to assist in the arrival/departure of a ship from a port
Rating	A seafarer who has functions only at the support level
Royal Navy	The United Kingdom's armed naval shipping force
Stevedore	A locally engaged port worker employed to load or discharge the cargo

INTRODUCTION

1

This book is about women seafarers employed on board today's world merchant ships. It covers women recruited from both developed and developing countries employed in the commercial and cruise sectors.[1] Although the employment of women in the industry involves many dimensions, this book focuses on the following aspects: the participation level of women in the industry; policies concerning women's maternity and employment rights; and women seafarers' experiences with regard to their recruitment, training and maternity leave as well as work and life at sea generally.

After the historical background and contemporary context to the study have been set out in Chapter 2, Chapter 3 presents the findings of the SIRC/ILO Survey on female participation rates. Chapter 4 then examines the practices and policies of national and international regulatory agencies, employers, trade unions and maritime education and training (MET) institutions. The experiences of women seafarers who participated in the study are described in detail in Chapter 5. The report concludes with a series of recommendations in Chapter 6.

Objectives

The research presented here was commissioned by the ILO following the resolution concerning women seafarers adopted by the 29th Session of the Joint Maritime Commission, 22–26 January 2001, in Geneva, and was conducted by the SIRC, Cardiff University (United Kingdom). Primarily, the

---

[1] Given that, until the 1990s, seafaring has been a predominantly male industry, the literature on maritime labour has had little to say on women except as dependent relatives (Dana, 1925; Lane, 1986, 1990; Chapman, 1992). Since the 1990s, however, feminist historians (Stark, 1998; Creighton and Norling, 1996; Fournier, 1993; Dugaw, 1992) have begun to examine maritime history, although they have necessarily focused on very small numbers of women seafarers and make little reference to women employed in the world's merchant fleet today.

study is intended to provide an objective profile of the workforce from a gender perspective and to identify the main issues concerning the recruitment and retention of women seafarers. Emphasis is placed on explaining the current low participation rate of women in the labour market. Based on the research findings, recommendations are made to the major stakeholders in the world maritime industry with regard to furthering the integration of women on board the world's ships in the twenty-first century and increasing participation rates. Specifically, the study measures the participation rate of women seafarers in the workforce; examines the main issues surrounding the recruitment and retention of women; identifies existing good practice; and recommends measures that may further help the integration of women into shipboard communities.

The SIRC carried out an extensive programme of interviews with maritime regulators, the lecturers and principals of maritime academies, shipowners and ship managers, and trade union officers from 45 organizations and with 56 women seafarers in 13 countries in Asia, Europe and Latin America. Additional data were collected from a questionnaire survey that was responded to by 79 organizations from 34 countries, including 371 women sailing aboard 14 cruise ships, employed in two major cruise companies, between October and November 2001. Data were also drawn from the SIRC Global Labour Market Database and from several other SIRC research projects, in particular its research work on women employed in the cruise sector.

Methodology

The project collected data from four samples:

- a questionnaire survey of a range of stakeholder organizations – maritime education and training institutions (METs), regulatory agencies, trade unions and shipping companies (Number = 79);

- in-depth audio-taped interviews with key individuals in these stakeholder organizations (43);

- a questionnaire survey of women seafarers employed on 14 cruise ships operated by two different shipping companies (371);

- in-depth audio-taped interviews and focus groups with a range of women seafarers and cadets from 13 different countries, recruited via METs, employers, unions and missions to seafarers (56).

In addition, the project drew on continuing and recently completed research at the SIRC, most notably Zhao's (1998) study of women seafarers in the European Community, Zhao's research on seafarers on cruise ships[2] and the SIRC's Global Labour Market studies of cruise and cargo ships (based on crew lists from ships calling at ports in the Americas, Asia, Australasia and Europe).

It will be appreciated that there is no international sampling frame of seafarers from which a representative sample can be drawn. Therefore, in order to minimize bias, the project took samples from a wide range of sources – different organizations, different countries (developed and developing nations), different ranks and different industrial sectors. Furthermore, the project employed a number of methods (quantitative and qualitative) to ensure that an appropriate mix of data was collected, documenting socio-demographic profiles, employment practices and the policies of companies and trade unions on the one hand, and the personal experiences of women seafarers on the other hand. Details of the content of the questionnaires and interview schedules can be found in the Appendices.

The data were collected by a research team of five that included men and women from both developed and developing countries.

---

[2] The report is due to be published in September 2003.

BACKGROUND

2

Although women have participated in seafaring for some time, the employment of women in merchant shipping in relatively large numbers is a new phenomenon, dating only from the 1990s. This chapter looks at the historical background and the contemporary context concerning the employment of women at sea.

Women seafarers in history

For centuries, maritime history and literature have treated seafaring as a solely male domain. And although women have now begun to appear in maritime scholarship, they are mostly on the periphery, as stiff and objectified as the wooden figurehead that faced the sea on the bows of sailing ships. A few women have been recorded as having travelled as stewardesses, explorers or as companions to captains, but, on the whole, women did not take part in the actual running of ships (Creighton and Norling, 1996; Stanley, 1987).

It was not until the steamship era around 1900 that women began to be systematically recruited as crew members aboard passenger ships, admittedly in such service roles as children's nurses, stewardesses for women passengers travelling unaccompanied by men and as laundresses.

However, there are occasional examples of women holding significant positions on board ships. A Scottish woman who regularly sailed with her husband, the owner–master of a sailing ship, learned how to navigate and, on the death of her husband, became captain of the vessel. On her return to shore, she established, and was principal of, a successful nautical academy in Aberdeen. Then there was the legendary Victoria Drummond (Drummond, 1999), who was awarded the Order of the British Empire (OBE) for brave conduct while serving as an engineer with the British Blue Funnel Line in the Second World War. Once the war was over, she was unable to find employment as a chief engineer on British ships, and sailed for many years as a chief engineer on

5

Greek-owned vessels. There are other cases of women having served during the Second World War, mainly as radio officers aboard Allied ships, although they were few in number and exceptional. The former Soviet Union is an extraordinary anomaly. Reportedly, as many as 8,000 women served on the country's ocean-going merchant vessels and 21,000 on vessels employed in inland navigation during the Second World War (*La marine merchande en guerre*, undated). Even more unusual is the case of the woman captain of a Soviet ship that ran Arctic convoys. These women may have been exceptional, but they also showed what women could do when given the chance.

It was not until the post-1945 period that women began to appear regularly as crew members aboard cargo ships, most often on Swedish ships as stewardesses, cooks and radio officers. In Norway, 40 per cent of people training to be radio officers, or "wireless operators" as they were referred to in the mid-1950s, were women (*Fairplay*, 2003). But only in the late 1960s were women first recruited as officer cadets and this was mainly in response to the drop in numbers of young male recruits in Europe. At about the same time, during China's Cultural Revolution (1966–76), Chinese women seafarers crewed the world's first women-officer-only cargo ship, the *Fengtao*, which traded in international waters.[1] However, important though these instances may have been as pioneering steps, the fact remains that companies still preferred to hire men.

From the mid-1980s and for a period of about 15 years, the shipping world lost interest in recruiting women. This was primarily because the industry was overwhelmed with the mounting problems of flagging out, overcapacity and declining freight rates as well as having a new source of male seafarers – from Asia and Europe (ILO, 2001). Women continued to be recruited as officer cadets in Europe, but, since the overall number of seafarers being trained in this region was declining, no *particular* interest was attached to recruiting women. It was not until the late 1990s, when the industry began to experience serious difficulty in recruiting men as seafarers, did attention turn once more to women.

Focus on recruitment

Since the late 1990s, there has been a growing interest in training and recruiting women seafarers. This is largely connected to perceived shortages of officers in the world fleets. The latest Baltic and International Maritime Council (BIMCO) and the International Shipping Federation (ISF) report

---

[1] The impact of this episode has been such that shipowners, seafarers' trade unions and government and party officials in China referred to this ship and its crew every time the subject of women seafarers was raised by SIRC researchers. Given that there is very little literature on women seafarers and that the SIRC team has exhausted the few works available, it is reasonable to assume that the *Fengtao* is the only known ship in which women made up the majority of the crew.

suggests that the current shortage of officers corresponds to 4 per cent of the total officer workforce (16,000 officers) and predicts a 12 per cent shortfall (46,000 officers) by the year 2010 (IER, 2000). At some regional and national levels, the crisis has been particularly strongly felt, with the European Union (EU) facing serious problems. In its *Communication* delivered to the Council and the Parliament on 4 June 2001, the European Commission reported an estimated shortage of some 13,000 officers in 2001, rising to around 36,000 officers by 2006 (European Commission, 2001).[2]

There is undoubtedly an urgent need to recruit and retain more seafarers and the immediate prognosis is not good, since recruitment and training are already inadequate to meet existing demand. In the United Kingdom, where the recruitment level of cadets stands at around 400 a year, a recent study has indicated that shipping companies will need to train 1,200 cadets a year in order to maintain future requirements on board ships (MCA, 2000). In China, a country with an apparently abundant labour supply, shipowners have been so frustrated by the increasing difficulty in recruiting seafarers from traditional sources, that is, from port cities and the coastal provinces,[3] that the country has begun recruiting women to remedy the problem. The same interest has been expressed by the International Maritime Organization (IMO), which noted, in 1997, that women are an "under-utilized and under-developed resource which could provide part of the solution to the problem of crewing the future world merchant fleets" (IMO, 1997, p. 3).

One area in which attracting staff, albeit hotel and catering personnel, is not a problem is the cruise sector. With an average growth rate of 9.6 per cent, the fleet expanded tenfold in tonnage between 1970 and the late 1990s (ISL, 1998; Wild, 1999). It has been estimated that the sector employed some 92,000 seafarers in 2000 (ILO, 2001), of which about 70 per cent comprise hotel and catering staff. If all current orders of new vessels materialize, there will be a potential labour demand in the cruise sector for as many as 168,000 seafarers by 2004 (Wild, 1999).

However, despite the demand for staff in cruise shipping, the special nature of employment in this sector for hotel and catering personnel – long working hours, dependence on "tips" as wage supplements, crowded living space, the attendant lack of privacy and inadequate recreational facilities, the lack of pension and other social security arrangements – leaves the industry with a high labour turnover, which it shares with the hotel industry ashore, but which is arguably more serious aboard ship where retaining staff familiar with

---

[2] With this *Communication*, the European Commission provides an update on the decline in the number of EU seafarers, an analysis of the reasons behind the decline, the implications for the EU shipping community and the measures necessary to reverse it.

[3] This problem was reported to SIRC researchers by senior managers from Chinese shipping companies.

complex accommodation layouts is critically important in the event of emergencies. The average length of stay of hotel-sector crew members halved from three years in 1970 to 18 months in 1990 and was estimated to have halved again in 2000 (Zhao, 2001; Peisley, 1996).

It is against this background of a serious shortage of qualified seafarers in the marine sector and the high turnover of crew in hotel and catering that shipping companies have begun to turn to women as an alternative labour source for the industry.

Focus on gender

The increased interest in, and the actual growth of, the number of women seafarers in world shipping since the late 1990s is also the result of an important change in political direction.

Since the late 1970s, the United Nations has been promoting women's employment and the integration of women into all levels of political, economic and social development. In line with this, the IMO produced a strategy for integrating women into the maritime sector in 1988, when it began to implement its Women in Development (WID) programme, concentrating on equal access to maritime training through both mainstream programmes and gender-specific projects (IMO, 1988, 1992, 1997). One of the immediate impacts of the programme has been the rise in the percentage of women students taking part in the highest level of maritime training. For example, data collected for the SIRC/ILO Survey have revealed that, in 1995, women students made up less than 8 per cent of the total number of students at the World Maritime University (WMU); by 2001, this had risen to 21 per cent of the university's total student population. This achievement has been described as being "of pivotal importance" in the report of an impact assessment exercise carried out in December 2000,[4] although the potential of women seafarers has, in general, attracted remarkably little attention from commentators and policy-makers.

There have been two further commitments concerning women seafarers, made by the ILO and the IMO. The resolution adopted by the Joint Maritime Committee at its 29th Session, 22–26 January 2001, in Geneva, and the resolution adopted by the IMO at its 21st Session in 1999, and reiterated at the 50th Session of its Technical Cooperation Committee, 21 June 2001, called for a more active role to be taken in promoting the integration of women into the industry. In particular, the ILO's Joint Maritime Committee has called for more research to be conducted on women seafarers (ILO, 2001; IMO, 1997, 2001), and the present study is a response to this.

---

[4] See IMO, 2001.

WOMEN SEAFARERS' PARTICIPATION IN WORLD SHIPPING   3

Numbers and distribution

Overall, the participation rate of women in seafaring remains low. It has been estimated that women represent only 1 to 2 per cent of the world's 1.25 million seafarers and that most of these women are from developed countries.[1] This estimation still seems valid, even though the female participation rates in the seagoing workforce vary greatly by region, country, company and sector. By far the largest numbers of women, both absolutely and proportionately, are found in the hotel staffs of passenger ships (which includes both cruise ships and ferries).

Among a group of eight European countries (Belgium, Denmark, Finland, Germany, Italy, Norway, Sweden and the United Kingdom), the average proportion of women in the total seafaring workforce was found to be 9.15 per cent (see table 1), although the relatively high numbers of Swedish and Danish women and the very low numbers of Italian women seafarers seriously distort this average.

In other parts of the world, women's representation in the seafaring workforce also varies greatly from country to country. Their share of the workforce is 5 per cent in Latvia and Indonesia, about 3 per cent in Australia and 0.5 per cent in New Zealand (Effective Change Pty Ltd, 1995). In 1998, India reported that the country had 43,000 registered seafarers, which included only three women.[2] By the end of 2002, it was reported that "despite being a major supplier of seafarers to the international market, India has produced just a dozen female seafarers so far" (*Fairplay*, 2002). In the

---

[1] The estimate was first made by the IMO (1992). Although the BIMCO/ISF study regularly reports on the worldwide supply and demand of seafarers, it unfortunately makes no references to women seafarers (IER, 1995, 2000).

[2] This information was gathered by SIRC researchers during their fieldwork in India for the Maritime Communications (MARCOM) project in 1998.

Table 1   Distribution of women seafarers in a selection of European countries,
various years (1997–2001)

Country	No. of seafarers	Women seafarers	Women as a % of total
Sweden[a]	15 117	3 518	23.3
Denmark[b]	9 809	1 478	15.1
Norway[c]	20 352	2 016	10.0
United Kingdom[d]	14 442	1 202	8.3
Finland[e]	5 218	294	5.6
Belgium[f]	1 350	60	4.4
Germany[g]	10 415	434	4.2
Italy[h]	25 000	300	1.2
Totals	**101 703**	**9 302**	**9.15**

Notes: [a] Swedish Seafarers' Register, 1997; [b] Keitsch, 1997, pp. 50–51; [c] Norwegian Maritime Directorate, 2001; [d] IER, 2000; [e] SIRC Women Archive, 1998; [f] Federal Ministry of Employment and Labour, 1997; [g] Ministry of Transport, Germany, 2001; [h] Federation of Italian Transport Workers' Union, 1998.

Source: Zhao, 1998; SIRC/ILO Survey, 2001.

Table 2   Women seafarers employed in cargo shipping companies, 2001

Company	Country/region	Total seafarers	Women seafarers
A	Portugal	61	4 (6.55%)
B	Germany	900	7 (0.77%)
C	United Kingdom	1 395	7 (0.5%)
D	Bermuda	2 401	1 (0.04%)
E	Hong Kong (China)	2 898	1 (0.03%)
Totals		**7 655**	**20 (0.26%)**

Source: SIRC/ILO Survey, 2001.

Philippines, the largest supplier of seafarers to the world merchant fleet, only 225 women out of 230,000 seafarers appear on the national seafarers' register for 1983–90 (IMO, 1997). According to the SIRC/ILO Survey, in Brazil there are 1,279 women seafarers, out of a total of 119,835 seafarers, that is, 1.1 per cent of the workforce.

The SIRC/ILO Survey received 37 replies from cargo shipping companies registered in various parts of the world, most of them from Organisation for Economic Co-operation and Development (OECD) countries. These companies employ a total of 27,541 seafarers, of whom 212 (0.76 per cent) are women. Table 2 lists a sample of the companies that employ women in their cargo fleets.

Table 3   Women seafarers aboard cruise ships, 2000

Ship	Total crew	Men	Women	Women as a %
A	222	158	66	29.7
B	540	396	145	26.8
C	546	405	141	25.8
D	540	404	136	25.2
E	988	777	211	21.4
F	559	462	97	17.4
G	988	833	155	15.7
H	878	763	115	13.1
I	155	148	7	4.5
Totals	5 416	4 346	1 073	19.8

Source: SIRC Seafarers Database, 2000.

In China, a shipping company with one of the world's largest fleets (a labour force of 40,000 seafarers) and once internationally known for its women-officers-only vessel, the *Fengtao*, employs 150 women seafarers, all of whom work as hotel staff on passenger ships. This company ceased employing women on its cargo ships in the 1980s.[3]

The great majority of the world's women seafarers are employed aboard passenger ships. According to the SIRC Seafarers Database, in 2000 women accounted for over 18 per cent of the total seafaring labour force in the cruise fleet,[4] although the proportion of women on individual vessels varies from ship to ship, as table 3 shows. The findings of the SIRC/ILO Survey confirm this figure: on the cruise ships covered by the survey, there was a total complement of 5,300 seafarers on board of which 940 (17.7 per cent) were women.

According to the SIRC/ILO Survey, the highest participation rate for women is found in passenger shipping – 94 per cent compared with only 6 per cent employed on cargo ships. However, as figure 1 shows, if passenger shipping is broken down into cruise and ferry ship types, 68 per cent of all the women (3,554) whose companies participated in the survey work on ferries and 26 per cent on cruise ships. Generally, it seems that women in the ferry sector are recruited nationally or regionally and, like women employed on cruise ships, work mainly in the hotel and catering sector.

An additional indicator of female participation rates is women's membership in trade unions and this, too, shows low levels of representation.

[3] Fieldwork notes made by SIRC researcher Minghua Zhao, 1998–2001.

[4] This figure applies to women serving on board cruise ships only and does not include those working on board ferries.

Figure 1   Employment of women by ship type

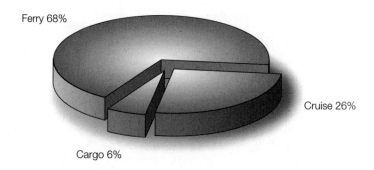

Ferry 68%

Cruise 26%

Cargo 6%

Table 4   Women's representation in seafarers' trade unions, 2001

Trade union[a]	Country	Total seafarers	Women seafarers	Women as a % of total
ESIU	Estonia	1 078	535	49.6
SEKO	Sweden	8 937	3 380	37.8
NSU	Norway	12 050	2 550	21.2
CAWU	Canada	1 399	249	17.8
BTB	Belgium	1 123	135	12.0
RMT	United Kingdom	6 287	469	7.5
SINCOMAR	Portugal	741	27	3.6
IOMMP	United States	5 998	210	3.5
FETCM	Spain	3 915	135	3.4
NZOU	New Zealand	412	14	3.4
NUMAST	United Kingdom	14 184	180	1.26
NMOA	Norway	5 961	62	1.04
PSU	Poland	5 210	46	0.9
NMS	Poland	6 955	50	0.7
Totals		**74 250**	**8 042**	**10.8**

Note: [a] See list of abbreviations (p. xiii) for full titles.

Source: SIRC/ILO Survey, 2001.

Although the membership registers of unions rarely cover all the women and men in the seafaring workforce, the low proportion of female members confirms the data from other sources as indicated above. Of the 27 trade unions that responded to the SIRC/ILO Survey, 13 reported that they had no data on women members. This may indicate that they do not differentiate between male and female members. Of the unions with data, women accounted for 11 per cent of the total membership (see table 4).

Figure 2   WMU enrolment by year of admission

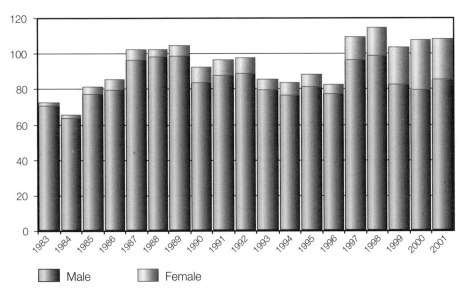

Source: WMU, 2001.

Despite the increasing numbers of women students undergoing maritime training at the highest level, as noted in Chapter 2, the number and proportion of women cadets or students enrolled in MET institutions confirm overall low participation rates. Even at the WMU, where the IMO's WID programme has been actively promoted with relatively successful results in recent years, the student population is still overwhelmingly male, as figure 2 shows.

The ratio of male to female students at marine and nautical schools was reported in 1998 as being 95:5 in the Netherlands and 96:4 in both Germany and the United Kingdom (Zhao, 1998). The SIRC/ILO Survey shows that the range of women's enrolment rates in MET institutions varies greatly between countries (see table 5).

There are some interesting and potentially significant emerging trends in several regions throughout the world. Where they are able to do so, some MET institutions have taken steps to increase the enrolment numbers of women. China's Shanghai Maritime University (SMU) has changed its traditional recruitment policy in response to the increasing difficulty the university was having in filling its School of Merchant Shipping with suitably qualified men and has, since 2000, been enrolling women. The decision made the headlines of some major national newspapers in China and was reported as a "historic breakthrough" (Tao and Zhou, 2000). Between 2000 and 2001, the university took on 49 women students (23 per cent of the total), all of whom are being trained as deck officers. In Spain, women seafarers were still

Table 5   Women students enrolled in MET institutions, 2001

MET institution[a]	Country	Total students	Women students	Women as a % of total
FNB	Spain	500	125	25.0
SMU[b]	China	210	49	23.0
CIAGA	Brazil	507	116	22.8
ITUMF	Turkey	148	26	17.6
AMA	Belgium	351	47	13.4
TUMM	Japan	377	47	12.5
FMST	Slovenia	223	27	12.1
ENMM	France	363	34	9.3
SMS	Sweden	321	20	6.2
CMU	Romania	707	39	5.5
SIMA	Denmark	1 618	78	4.8
ENIDH	Portugal	299	14	4.7
GCMS	United Kingdom	325	15	4.6
Totals		**5 703**	**641**	**10.8**

Note: [a] See list of abbreviation (p. xiii) for full titles. [b] These figures include first- and second-year students, that is, all the students enrolled since the university's no-women policy was dropped in 2000.

Source: SIRC/ILO Survey, 2001.

considered a "new subject" as recently as the mid-1990s, and the Spanish merchant navy has only been employing women since the first half of the 1980s (Rodriguez-Martos, 1995). In Barcelona, the University of Catalonia introduced the Dona programme in 1997 to encourage female students to enrol in its technical courses. The Faculty of Nautical Science (FNB) has benefited significantly from the new policy: women already account for 25 per cent of all students, in comparison with only 5 per cent in 1996. Similar cases have been found in other regions of the world. In Brazil, Rio de Janeiro's maritime academy, CIAGA, recruited 63 students for MET training in 2000, including 29 men and 34 women – all to be trained as deck officers. And in India a government order dated 1 October 2002 decreed that all public-sector MET institutions reduce their course fees for women by 50 per cent in order to encourage more women to choose a seafaring career. All privately run training institutes have been requested to "follow suit" (*Fairplay*, 2002).

The proportion of women among the teaching and research staff at MET institutions indirectly reflects the dominance of men in the maritime labour force. Of the 12 maritime schools and colleges surveyed in Germany and the United Kingdom in 1998, women accounted for 7.2 per cent of the total teaching staff (Zhao, 1998). By comparison, women made up 24 per cent of the total number of lecturers in German colleges and universities in 1998.[5] In the United Kingdom, female lecturers made up 38 per cent of the total teaching staff in the country's higher education institutions and 48 per cent in further and higher education colleges (HESA, 1997).[6]

Position in the ship's hierarchy

Where the seagoing workforce is concerned, there is a high concentration of women in the hotel personnel of cruise ships, employed mostly in rating grades, regardless of sector. As shown in the following charts, among the women seafarers covered by the SIRC/ILO Survey, 7 per cent are officers and the rest (3,305 or 93 per cent) are ranked as ratings (see figure 3). By comparison, 42 per cent of male seafarers are officers and 58 per cent are ratings (see figure 4).

Figure 3   Female distribution by rank

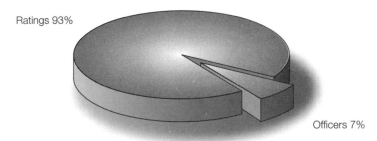

Ratings 93%

Officers 7%

Source: SIRC/ILO Survey, 2001.

Figure 4   Male distribution by rank

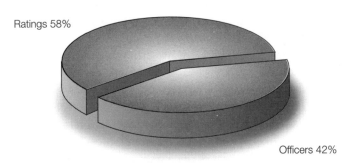

Ratings 58%

Officers 42%

Source: SIRC/ILO Survey, 2001.

---

[5] Federal Statistical Office Germany, 2001, Fachserie 11, Reihe 4.4, table 4, pp. 23–24.

[6] The information from the National Association of Teachers in Further and Higher Education (NATFHE) was provided in a telephone interview in 1998.

Figure 5   Occupational segregation by gender: A comparison

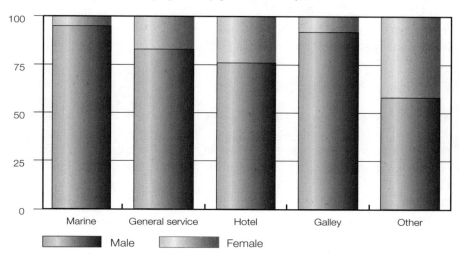

Source: Graph reconstructed using data drawn from Zhao, 2001.

Most women seafarers, regardless of nationality, are employed in the hotel sector. Germany is a good example in this respect. Although there are several German female shipmasters, women cooks and waitresses make up more than 21 per cent of all catering personnel (Keitsch, 1997, p. 50). In the United Kingdom, the Chamber of Shipping (COS) *Manpower Inquiry* of 1995 found that 88.4 per cent of female seafarers aboard all vessels fell within the category of hotel ratings, whereas cadets and officers accounted for only 11.6 per cent of the total.

There are, of course, women working at the top of the ship hierarchy, although their numbers are small. Among the 1,500 German masters in 1998, for example, there were only three women (Casagrande, 1999) and between 1998 and 2000 there were only two female captains among the 78 cruise ships sampled in the SIRC Seafarers Database (2000).

The situation on cruise ships is quite different. There has been a clear rise in the proportion of women employed in the sector and more women have been appointed to such key positions as pursers, cruise directors, financial controllers, housekeepers, food and beverage managers, chefs and executive chefs. Among hotel staff more women are being appointed in management and supervisory posts and this seems likely to continue. Although most of the doctors on cruise ships are currently men and most of the nurses are women, the rise in the number of women doctors and male nurses ashore is bound to be reflected soon aboard cruise ships. More women are also likely to be appointed in the more routine service tasks of the hotel sector. Very few women are employed in the marine department of cruise ships. Figure 5 shows that women are concentrated in the

Figure 6   Female distribution by region of origin (hotel sector)

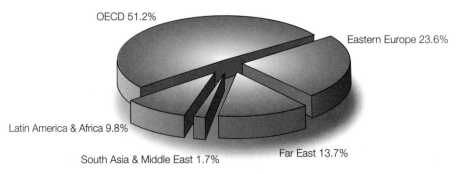

Source: Lane et al., 2002.

Figure 7   Male distribution by region of origin (hotel sector)

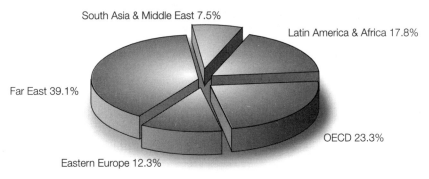

Source: Lane et al., 2002.

hotel and other ("non-technical") sectors of ships as cabin stewardesses, waitresses, cleaners or utility workers, and their representation in the marine and galley departments is extremely low (Zhao, 2001). Like the marine department on ships, the galley remains largely a male preserve, although there are clear indications from company human resource (HR) managers that this is changing. It remains uncertain, however, whether the number of women working in the marine department will increase. There is little doubt that cruise ship operators are, in general, keen to appoint more women officers, but current policies are too restricted to OECD nationalities to make that a strong possibility: there are simply too few women cadets being recruited and trained.

What are the origins of women seafarers (see figures 6, 7 and 8)? As figure 6 shows, OECD countries recruit the largest proportion of women employed on cruise ships (51.2 per cent), followed by Eastern Europe (23.6 per cent), the Far East (13.7 per cent), Latin America and Africa (9.8 per cent) and South Asia and the Middle East (1.7 per cent). It is worth noting that the

Figure 8   Comparison of gender distribution by region of origin

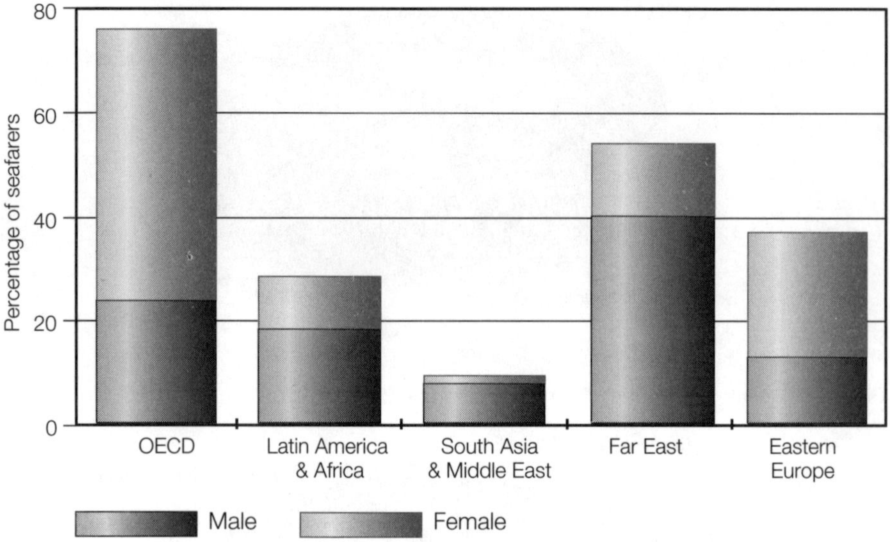

Source: Lane et al., 2002.

regional composition of the female workforce differs significantly from that of the male workforce. Most male seafarers are recruited from the Far East (39.1 per cent), followed by 23.3 per cent from OECD countries, 17.8 per cent from Latin America and Africa, 12.3 per cent from Eastern Europe, and 7.5 per cent from South Asia and the Middle East (Lane et al., 2002).

Such a difference between the regional composition of men and women seafarers reflects at least two issues that play an important role in the stratification of the labour market in cruise shipping. First, it reveals the industry's efforts to match its labour force to those of Europeans and North Americans employed as front-line workers in the hotel industry on land, hence the higher representation of women seafarers in this sector. Second, it shows the constraints the industry is facing in recruiting women from certain regions. For example, in some Asian countries, women are not encouraged to take employment away from home and working on a ship is considered unacceptable.

The age profile of women seafarers

What is the average age of women employed on cruise ships? An initial analysis of the age profiles of seafarers indicates that the mean age is 33.2 for all seafarers, 35.4 for men and 31.5 for women. In other words, women crew members are, on average, four years younger than their male colleagues, as figures 9 and 10 show.

Figure 9   Age profile of male seafarers

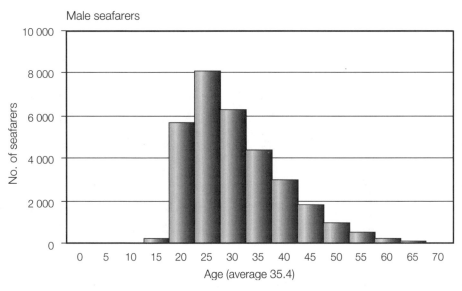

Source: SIRC Seafarers Database.

Figure 10   Age profile of female seafarers

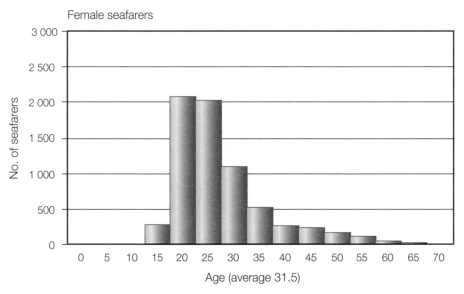

Source: SIRC Seafarers Database.

Figure 11   Age comparison by gender and region (hotel sector)

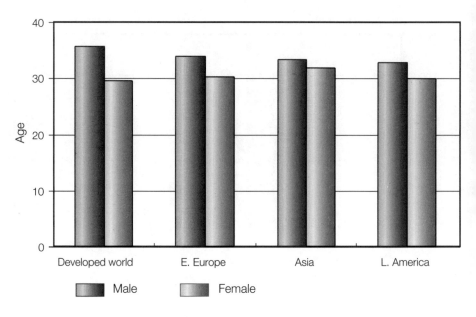

Source: SIRC Seafarers Database.

Figure 12   Gender distribution by age profile (hotel sector)

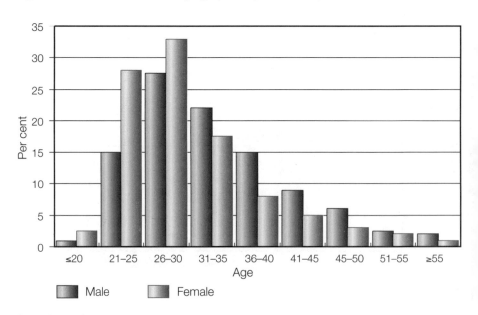

Source: Lane et al., 2002.

In the hotel sector, the average age of men in both developed and developing countries is significantly higher than that of women (figure 11). This seems to indicate that the industry prefers to employ younger women in the hotel sector, which has been confirmed by the findings of our field research. In China and the Philippines, for example, the age limits set by many crewing agents are substantially lower for women than for men.

Taking one specific work area, the hotel sector on cruise vessels for example, proportionally more women are found in the under-30 age groups and, in comparison, more men in the 30-plus age groups, as figure 12 shows (Lane et al., 2002). Clearly, the hotel sector prefers to employ younger women.

Summary

This chapter presented an overall view of women's participation in seafaring in various countries, regions and sectors. It was found that women remain a minority despite the rise in their numbers in the past decade or so.

In commercial shipping, the level of women's representation is extremely low. Most women working in this sector come from developed countries and are employed as cadets or officers. It is worth noting that a relatively substantial number of women have recently been admitted into MET institutions in several regions of the world and are currently undergoing training as future deck officers or engineers. Two factors are particularly important in determining the future participation rate of women in this sector: first, whether shipping companies employ women once they have completed their training; and second, whether MET institutions throughout the world are really committed to taking on more women students.

Most women seafarers work in the passenger sector, on ferries and cruise ships. Most of the women in the ferry sector, which has the highest participation level of women, are recruited on a regional basis and work in the hotel and catering sector. Given the rapid growth of the ferry sector and the nature of the trade, it can be reasonably predicted that employment of women in this part of the industry is likely to continue to grow, although the role of women aboard may not see any real changes.

Since the late 1990s, there has been a significant rise in the number of women employed in cruise shipping. As in ferry shipping, women on cruise ships are, for the most part, found in the hotel and catering sector. However, women seafarers in the cruise sector are recruited on a worldwide basis and increasingly from Asia, Eastern Europe and other developing countries. Despite the slowdown of the world economy since 11 September 2001, cruise shipping remains robust and strong (Belcher and Winchester, 2002). The recent restructuring of the market, such as the redeployment of the fleet and tightened security at some American ports, is unlikely to change the nature of the industry or the nature of seafarers' labour aboard. The high crew turnover is, therefore, likely to continue, hence the continuous high demand for seafarers, including women.

The overall demand for women seafarers is likely to continue to grow in all sectors. However, their recruitment and, in particular, their retention do not depend on market demand alone. It is the employment policies of shipping companies, seafarers' trade unions, maritime regulating agencies, at both national and international levels, and, more importantly, the implementation of these policies by these organizations that will determine whether women join and then remain within the shipping industry. Fundamentally, it is the experiences of women in the workplace as well as their evaluation and interpretation of such experiences that define the quality of their employment and will determine their future at sea. These issues are explored and analysed in the next two chapters.

THE MARITIME INDUSTRY: POLICIES AND PRACTICES

4

Introduction

This chapter examines the policies and practices of those institutions and organizations which, when taken together, determine the shape and character of the labour market for seafarers generally and, therefore, for women seafarers in particular. In the first instance, it is, of course, employers who determine the key features of the labour market. As buyers of labour power, they decide who is, and who is not, considered suitable for employment. Any actual, perceived or potential labour shortages will inevitably lead employers to assess new sources of labour; it was precisely such considerations that, in the late 1960s and early 1970s, led employers in the then dominant maritime countries to develop systematic policies for recruiting women.

The previously haphazard and contingent employment policies for women at sea aboard cargo ships (typically radio officers, cooks and stewardesses married to male officers) demonstrated that women had the capacity to be effective seafarers. However, the new *organized* approach led to the development of formal policies, acknowledging that women could, and should, be considered on the same basis as men – but mainly in officer ranks. Apart from a few "experiments" with all-women catering staff on cargo ships, there had been no systematic attempts to recruit women ratings for the merchant fleets of developed market economy countries.

Because of declining recruitment and retention rates among men, companies in developed market economies had no choice but to consider women as possible employees. In doing so, they received political encouragement, which incorporated an increasing awareness that there were few, if any, occupations in which women were incapable of participating. In centrally planned economies, by contrast, most notably in China, political considerations were much more prominent in informing policies on women's employment. In the former Soviet bloc, and particularly in the former Soviet Union, labour supply considerations were by no means absent from policies concerned with the recruitment of women for the fishing, whaling and merchant shipping fleets.

Women have worked aboard passenger ships since the nineteenth century but were not recruited in significant numbers in the cruise sector of the industry until the late 1980s, when the numbers of women working on board cruise ships increased in line with employment patterns in the shore-based hotel and catering industry.

Once employers have introduced new labour recruitment policies, other labour-related institutions inevitably respond. In the shipping industry, pluralism is pervasive, and often more in international than in national arenas. Diplomacy, therefore, "requires" employers to consult and "negotiate" with national and international regulators, training providers and trade unions. Where women seafarers are concerned, once recruited they immediately have to go through training and certification procedures that involve prolonged contact with MET professionals. These professionals are inevitably influential, first because they are the first significant members of the shipping world to whom the new recruits are exposed and, second, because MET professionals feed their experiential knowledge of women recruits back to employers as well as forwarding it on to successive cohorts of new recruits.

Often while still at MET institutions, or soon afterwards, new recruits are likely to join a trade union. They become familiar with trade union policies via publications but especially as a result of exposure and discussion among established seafarers. Many of the sorts of questions with which they become familiar are not just employer–employee issues but also matters concerned with national and international policies that are best regulated on a state or global basis. Thus, new recruits discover a world of employers, MET institutions, trade unions and national and international regulators, all of whom have a direct bearing on the policies and practices that have an impact on the quality of their lives. In this chapter, the role of these various bodies and organizations is examined.

International organizations

In the shipping industry, "government" is likely to be understood as being the IMO and the ILO. Both these regulatory bodies have become increasingly influential as the industry has reached out into areas where regulation is either thin or non-existent.

The International Maritime Organization

The most important development at the International Maritime Organization (IMO) regarding women has been the work of its Integrated Technical

Cooperation programme, which has mainly addressed the need to increase the employment of women from developing countries in the shipping industry ashore.

The following quotation is an extract from the IMO's *Strategy for the integration of women in the maritime sector* (1988):

> [The] IMO recognizes the integral role of women in the maritime field, both as agents and as beneficiaries in the development process. Thus, despite the highly specialized and technical nature of the maritime sector, which is still conceptualized as largely male-oriented, [the] IMO has adopted an advocacy role to encourage greater participation of women throughout the shipping and maritime industry.

In addition to its major interest in the employment of women in the industry ashore, the IMO has also demonstrated concern over the shortage of officers in the world fleet. In its *Strategy*, it states:

> Women currently only comprise some 1 to 2 per cent at most of the 1.2 million strong global workforce of seafarers, although technical improvements in shipboard operations are accelerating the access of women to employment within the maritime sector.

Furthermore, the same *Strategy* considers the integration of women as a condition for achieving sustainable development, made more acute because of the shortage of officers mentioned above.

The IMO produced its strategy for integrating women into the shipping industry in 1988. The then Secretary-General of the IMO designated a Focal Point for WID for the secretariat to develop and coordinate the implementation of strategies designed to enhance the participation and advancement of women in the industry. The WID programme became an integral part of the IMO's Integrated Technical Cooperation programme.

The Focal Point for WID began its work in 1989 with the implementation of an ad hoc programme of sensitization and recruitment measures. This programme was completed in 1992.

The first Medium-term plan for the integration of women in the maritime sector covered the period 1992–96 and was later revised to take into account the strategic focus and priority actions of the United Nations system-wide medium-term plan for the advancement of women 1996–2001. The Action programme for equal opportunities and advancement of women in the maritime sector 1997–2001 updated the previous Medium-term plan and its associated plan of action.[1] This second Action programme sought to:

---

[1] These programmes could only be conducted thanks to a special grant provided by Norway of US$250,000, covering the period 1991–2000. The grant financed a background study on the role of women in the maritime sector, the two action plans referred to above, two in-house gender training seminars, one regional seminar, two national seminars and 39 fellowships.

- integrate women into mainstream maritime activities;

- improve women's access to maritime training and technology;

- increase the percentage of women at senior management level within the maritime sector;

- consolidate the integration of women into the maritime sector as an integral element of the IMO's technical cooperation activities.

The International Labour Organization

International standards for the labour market of seafarers are established in the Conventions and Recommendations of the International Labour Organization.[2] One of the most important ILO maritime instruments is the Merchant Shipping (Minimum Standards) Convention, 1976 (No. 147). It embodies minimum standards on a wide range of maritime labour questions. In particular, the Convention requires the establishment of adequate procedures for the engagement of seafarers on ships registered in the territory of the ratifying country and for the investigation of complaints arising in that connection. It calls for regulations in areas of safety, hours of work and crewing, shipboard conditions of employment and shipboard living arrangements. Furthermore, the Convention empowers countries to investigate complaints concerning foreign ships calling in their ports and to remedy hazardous conditions on board.

The fundamental principle and right to non-discrimination on the grounds of sex is established in the Discrimination (Employment and Occupation) Convention, 1958 (No. 111), one of the eight core international labour standards. This Convention prohibits any direct or indirect gender discrimination with regard to vocational training, access to employment, terms and conditions of employment, promotion and termination of employment. The principle and right to non-discrimination was recently re-affirmed in the ILO's Declaration of Fundamental Principles and Rights and its Follow-Up in 1998. A list of international labour standards relevant to women workers' rights, including women seafarers, is contained in Appendix XII.

The ILO has identified gender as an issue that cuts across all its programmes and activities in the world of work. In 1999, the Director-General

---

[2] Thirty-nine maritime Conventions, 28 Recommendations and one Protocol have been adopted so far, covering a broad spectrum of aspects of maritime employment, including the conditions of access to maritime employment; training, recruitment and the placement of seafarers; the procedure for determining conditions of work, standards of hours of work, rest and holidays; repatriation; safety and health on board, and the accommodation of seafarers; the inspection of seafarers' working and living conditions, and the social security of seafarers.

of the ILO issued a policy statement highlighting a strong and visible political commitment to gender equality and gender mainstreaming at the highest level of the Office.

One of the ILO's main tools for promoting gender equality is in the area of standard setting and supervision. The ILO's standard-setting work in this area is based on two central concerns. The first is to guarantee equality of opportunity and treatment in access to training, employment, promotion, organization and decision-making, as well as securing equal terms and conditions of remuneration, benefits, social security and welfare services provided in connection with employment. The second is to protect women workers, especially in relation to conditions of work, which may entail risks during pregnancy.

ILO operational activities address equality principles and rights through advisory services, research, advocacy, training courses, worker education, workshops, meetings and within technical cooperation activities. In recent years, topics that have been the focus of ILO study and activities include: women in decision-making; maternity protection; equality; collective bargaining; equal remuneration for work of equal value; and sexual harassment.

In its ILO Sectoral Activities Programme, the report of the 29th Session of the Joint Maritime Commission, 2001, addressed gender issues in the maritime sector in relation to sexual harassment and accommodation issues. Point 3 of the agenda addressed the impact on seafarers' living and working conditions of changes in the structure of the shipping industry, the discussion of which was based on the SIRC report of the same name (ILO, 2001). The survey of women seafarers in some major EU countries as well as additional information on the female maritime labour force worldwide were presented at this session.[3]

Governments

The response rate from government agencies to the SIRC/ILO Survey was extremely low: replies from only four countries – one in Latin America, two in Western Europe and one in Eastern Europe – were received. SIRC researchers and collaborators were, however, able to gather a substantial amount of information from other countries, including China, Germany, Romania and Spain.

On employment questions, other than those relating to safe crewing levels, safety and certification compliance, the regulatory role is normally minimal, except in those cases where employers and trade unions, separately or jointly, look for assistance. This may be on matters of health and safety, where new legislation

---

[3] http://www.ilo.org/public/english/dialogue/sector/techmeet/jmc01/jmcr3.htm (10 Mar. 2003).

is required, or on training and educational matters, where subsidy or other support is sought. The situation does, of course, vary according to the extent to which individual states are characterized by more or less government involvement in economic and social regulations. Where international regulators are concerned, many states either send delegations, with representatives of employers' organizations and trade unions, to the IMO and the ILO or have employers' and trade union representatives brief and advise their delegations.

No evidence was found of any proactive activity by OECD governments in respect of women seafarers. In the cases we were able to examine, government activity is confined to identifying appropriate ways of ensuring that generic government policies relating to women are applied to women seafarers. In fact, all EU countries have in their legislation equal opportunities policies for men and women. In Germany, for example, the Government has no specific policy on women seafarers but it does have an equal opportunities policy, and the maritime administration, therefore, has an obligation to see that the provisions of this policy are applied to shipping. This instance serves as a good model for what is widely practised in other countries. In the United Kingdom, the Maritime and Coastguard Agency (MCA) published a *Marine Guidance Note* (MCA, 1997b) in which the relevant health and safety regulations for the protection of new and expectant mothers was laid out. These guidelines are derived from the Employment Rights Act, which applies throughout the United Kingdom. Similar instances can be found in Romania, where MET institutions have responded to government equal opportunities directives, and in Norway, where the Norwegian Maritime Directorate ensures that laws governing the employment of women are observed in the shipping industry.

As previously stated, the regulator's task is mostly to ensure the particular observance of universal rules. It is for these reasons that, when shipping employers and trade unions wish to ensure that legislation properly applies to their spheres of interest, they make their views known to administrative officials, while simultaneously finding ways of making direct representations to government ministers. Equally, the same general political practices apply in more centralized economies, although circuits of access to political power and influence are organized differently. Usually trade unions and employers have a common understanding of the political processes and so, with the inevitable exception of matters in which they are directly opposed, it is common for them to make joint representations.

Employers and trade unions have not always worked together, but one of the few occasions when employers and trade unions have taken on an active role of partnership has been on new employment issues related to women seafarers. In the United Kingdom, for example, in the 1970s, when leading British companies were beginning to recruit women cadets, both the General Council of British Shipping (GCBS) and the officers' union, the National Union of Maritime and Aviation Shipping Transport Officers (NUMAST), worked together to ensure that training and personnel safety questions were taken into consideration. Later, in 1981, NUMAST introduced the Victoria Drummond Award for High-achieving Women Seafarers, which was actively supported by shipping companies.

Employers

Shipping companies

Our survey of employers included 64 companies, of which six were in the cruise sector and 58 in the commercial sector. In-depth interviews were conducted with 22 senior executives representing shipowners and managers in Asia, Europe and North America, and 42 companies completed questionnaires.

Very few companies have specific policies regarding women, although that does not necessarily mean that they are opposed to the recruitment of women seafarers. One major cruise company, for example, has a large and predominantly female personnel department, which deals with marine crew, pursers, nurses and doctors. At the time of the survey, the head of department was a woman, and two of her female senior managers insisted that their company had a gender-blind policy:

> We just treat everybody on their own merits. All the policies are applied equally. We put our applicants through a two-day assessment programme. We have a residential centre for maybe six, eight, ten candidates and we put them all, male and female, through a number of tests – competency tests, personality tests, those sort of things. And we look at everybody on their individual merits, regardless of whether they're male or female. We don't have any active policies to prevent or encourage the promotion of women. But certainly being a team of women HR officers, we wouldn't stand in the way if we felt that a female officer warranted promotion. On a level with men, they would get the promotion. You have to remember we are predominantly female and we don't see ourselves as anything other than equal to our male colleagues, so why should we view our female crew members as anything other than equal to their male counterparts?

Only in some of its personnel practices was this company specifically attentive to gender issues. As one of the senior managers said:

> Some of our male officers are not as positive as we are about women in their team and, while we don't have any official policies, at a senior level we would try to avoid appointing a woman into the teams of some officers, knowing that the female officer might have a difficult time.

The personnel manager (male) of another large cruise-sector company spoke of a very similar policy with respect to marine crew and said that he employed female officers in both deck and engine departments. He said:

> Obviously with deck and technical officers, people are recruited on their qualifications and their experience with companies, so we treat male and female applicants in the same way. We also have an officer cadet programme, and at the moment we have three female deck cadets and one female engineer cadet.

Similar employment policies were found in the cargo-ship sector. A senior manager of a North European company revealed that on one occasion he had actually suggested to his in-house crewing agent that they should try a ship with an all-woman crew, but, as he said:

> The problem is to get the girls with the experience. So I wouldn't hesitate. If I have a good woman officer and if she's bright and good at her job, does everything to company rules, then why not as a master? But she must then also have the power to run the vessel. But there are many examples that this can happen. I think X [a named company] has women masters.

Shipowners and ship managers with experience of employing women were very positive about their performance and their impact aboard ships. A European shipowner with a fleet of more than 30 ships, mostly container vessels, has been employing women officers since the late 1970s and currently has two women masters with a third working ashore. He told us:

> The women are more alert. I hate to say they are more intelligent, because I don't make them do intelligence tests, but I see them as more engaged. With male masters, you do have good ones – some average and some even perhaps a little below average – but you employ them and they run the ships satisfactorily. But then maybe you have a special ship and you're a little bit afraid to put them there – but the women, they're above average.

The same shipowner went on to speak with some enthusiasm about the three women masters employed on board his ships. In describing some of their qualities, he gave the example of their voyage reports. Comparing the reports from his female and male masters, he explained:

> I see all the letters and if, let's say, she writes half a page of what's going on aboard the ship, I know exactly what is going on. But if some of the male masters write three pages, I still don't know what's going on. This female master, she comes to the point and has very good judgement about what's important.

A senior executive of one of the world's largest ship management companies made a similar point but more emphatically:

Since the 1960s, seafaring has become a different job. Nowadays, you don't need so many muscles, you don't need to be like Arnold Schwarzenegger. You must have good brains, and women are usually better in this respect.

Another European shipowner saw yet other advantages in having women officers. He argued that, with women aboard, the whole social atmosphere of a ship improves. He told us:

The advantage is that with women aboard the language is more positive. There is a "please" all of a sudden and even among the male community everything changes. There is no disadvantage in having women aboard. Only advantages.

By contrast, there were a number of European and Asian shipowners who were very negative about women seafarers – but none of them had ever employed women before. Thus, one can assume that their negative views are based on stereotypes and prejudices rather than on knowledge and experience. The sorts of negative views expressed were much the same whether they came from Asians or Europeans and are illustrated by the following quotes:

Women are OK for passenger ships.

We have had a few [female] cadets in my country, but they leave after two or three years.

We cannot solve the officer shortage with women. Women are women. I don't believe women can be good officers.

When women go aboard ship, they will find somebody, make love, maybe marry and then leave.

We should sit down and think about employing women. Is it necessary for a woman to be a pilot or a bosun? Why should she be a bosun? If it is just to show the chauvinist pigs that she can perform that role, then it is wrong. However, if it is because we are at war and women are needed, then I think it is necessary. There should be a reason. I have no problem with women working aboard a ship – but if the reason is just because of politics, then the answer should be "No".

These objections accurately represent the range of those we found at interview. However, between the most positive and negative attitudes expressed by employers there was inevitably a range of opinions relating to women seafarers, which translated into a variety of policies with regard to recruitment. Some companies actively discriminate against all women applicants, with three stating that they have a specific policy of excluding women in all posts. As justification, they cited their belief that women are incapable of heavy work and that they do not remain in the industry for very long. Others are prepared to employ women in some ranks but not others, excluding women from posts such as those of bosun and chief engineer. Occasionally "parent" companies might not discriminate against women, but crewing agents, who employ the staff, do. Some crewing agents remunerate men and women on an unequal basis, paying women less than men of equal rank. Companies who employ women across all ranks are sometimes disinclined to employ women of particular nationalities, and others are reluctant to place female European officers in positions of authority on ships with multinational crews. In general, where women are regarded as potential workers they are subjected to the same application procedures and forms of assessment as their male counterparts. However, in the cruise sector, there is some evidence that successful female applicants are expected to meet specific physical requirements conforming with idealized notions of "attractiveness".

Those companies employing women, in both the cruise and cargo sectors, reported a range of responses to the need for gender-related policies protecting women seafarers on board ship. In terms of family-related policies, companies across the industry tend not to differentiate between their male and female employees. Where the wives or partners of male seafarers are allowed to accompany them on board, so too are the husbands or partners of female seafarers, and with the same attendant conditions. Similarly, employers reported that they had the same policy for men and women in terms of dependent children joining vessels.

Most companies reported giving little thought to the purchase and disposal of sanitary products by their female employees at sea. This was particularly the case in the commercial sector of the industry, where women are largely expected to deal with such matters as they see fit. Few companies have any provision for the sale of feminine hygiene products on board through bonded stores. It was, however, reported that ships sailing with particular flags are required under the regulations of the States in which they are registered to carry a limited supply of sanitary products on board all their vessels.

Many shore-based companies have developed formal policies relating to sexual harassment and this applies equally to shipping companies which have generally adopted policies for their land-based staff. However, few companies in the commercial sector have such policies pertaining to their sea-based employees. In the cruise sector, policies on sexual harassment are more prevalent and some appeared to be fully comprehensive.

As with sexual harassment, company policy on the employment of pregnant women varies. In general, however, companies are opposed to allowing women seafarers to continue working while pregnant. Some reported that, in the event of a woman discovering she was pregnant, they would arrange for her to disembark, at her own expense. Others have more generous policies and will try to find pregnant women shore-based work. Yet others allow women to continue working on board, providing they can supply a medical certificate guaranteeing fitness for work.

Maternity benefits, as such, are rarely offered to women seafarers, who, in line with their male counterparts, are generally employed on short-term contracts on a voyage-by-voyage basis. However, women sailing on some non-flag-of-convenience ships are entitled to maternity benefits, under the prevailing laws of the relevant flag State.

Although the research uncovered a range of attitudes among employers, in essence these attitudes represent different versions of very traditional *conceptions* of male and female roles. At different times and in different places, there is ample evidence that women are able to perform the same sorts of tasks as men, and our research demonstrates that, so far as modern shipboard work is concerned, those shipowners who have employed women on board their vessels have found them to be, at the very least, the equals of men.

Employers' organizations

The ISF is an international employers' organization for ship operators. Members are made up of national shipowners' associations from over 30 countries around the world. The ISF represents the industry at inter-governmental level and deals with matters relating to personnel and employment. It is involved in the ILO's Joint Maritime Commission and has consultative status with the ILO, where it coordinates shipowners' representation at discussions of maritime standards. The ISF's concern with employment practices includes both male and female employees. However, to date, it has not addressed gender issues specifically. The low visibility of the issues faced by women seafarers is reflected in their recently published *Guidelines on good employment practice* (ISF, 2001). These *Guidelines* are based on the ILO's maritime Conventions and Recommendations and recognize good practice in the shipping industry. Issues covered include industrial relations, recruitment and personnel administration, general conditions of employment, health and safety and welfare. These *Guidelines* are seen to be equally applicable to male and female seafarers. However, they do not include any guidelines expressly relating to gender other than under "Discrimination and Abuse", where it is asserted that:

> Any physical, social or mental abuse, whether caused by discrimination on the basis of race, colour, religious affiliation or *gender* [...] should be prevented. (ISF, 2001, p. 14, emphasis added)

An ISF official suggested that this absence of specific guidance for international application does not indicate any lack of commitment to the implementation of policies relevant to the employment of women. Rather, he felt this reflected the very small number of women employed as seafarers in the international industry and the consequent low profile of gender issues in international discussions. At the national level, however, he stated that many national shipowners' associations have more specific policies regarding the employment of women reflecting the requirements of national law, and that many crew agreements, both national and international, contain clauses covering gender issues.

An example of an agreement in which specific attention has been given to women seafarers is the model agreement developed by the International Maritime Employers' Committee (IMEC) for use on open-register ships. Employers using this model are bound by clause 24 on maternity, which states that:

24.1 In the event that a crew member becomes pregnant during the period of employment:

(a) the seafarer shall advise the master as soon as the pregnancy is confirmed;

(b) the company will repatriate the seafarer as soon as reasonably possible but in no case later than the 26th week of pregnancy;

(c) the seafarer shall be entitled to two months' compensation in accordance with paragraph 19.4.

However, women working in the cruise sector are not covered by this agreement as IMEC membership extends only to those employers in the cargo sector (ITF, 2000).

Trade unions

Individual unions

While an organization such as the ITF has a coordinating and campaigning role, its affiliated member unions have some latitude in developing their own individual policies. In order to explore these various strategies, we collected data from seafarers' unions in different world regions. The data discussed here are based on 17 questionnaire responses from unions representing 47,556 seafarers from 15 countries. In addition, in-depth interviews were conducted with senior trade union officers from Asia and Europe.

Fewer than half (seven) of the unions that responded to the survey reported having an equal opportunities policy or any policy specifically relating to women. However, some trade unions reported well-defined policies on women seafarers and effective infrastructures for dealing with gender issues. A commitment to equal opportunities and anti-sexual harassment policies was evident among some of the unions.

Trade unions, particularly in Europe, reported difficulties in developing policies and campaigning on "women's issues" as a result of the pressures placed on them by increased levels of unemployment among their members – a consequence of reduced crewing levels, changes in labour recruitment strategies and flagging out. As one European official told us:

> To be honest, we haven't really discussed things like women aboard. You cannot really discuss these things when you see all these ships going out of your register.

In some circumstances some trade unionists may be suspicious of attempts to introduce women into the labour market when their inclusion threatens the jobs of existing members. They are less likely to be resistant in the context of expanding employment markets, as currently experienced in the cruise sector, and those where women are recruited on the same basis as men. NUMAST adapted fairly quickly to the training of women officers, as can be seen by the introduction of the Victoria Drummond Award, in 1981, for women making distinctive contributions to the union and the industry generally. The most recent recipient of the award is Margaret Pidgeon, who became the United Kingdom's first woman master in 1999.

In Asia, union attitudes to women are more ambivalent. In China, for example, many women who worked in waterborne transport and especially in river transport have in recent years been made redundant. Here, the union's main concern has been to secure retraining for its members. As one official told us:

> The focus of our attention has been on equal employment rights with regard to redundancy. Since companies always get rid of their women employees first, we have tried our best to support these women through retraining.

Generally, only a small number of sexual harassment cases have been reported to trade unions, and sexual harassment is not a priority of seafarers' trade unions in most countries. When asked about their policy focus, all unions listed issues of recruitment, training and ship-board working conditions. Only one stated that sexual harassment was a major concern. There appears to be little awareness among union leaders that few reports of sexual harassment do not necessarily indicate that sexual harassment is a rare occurrence. However, there have been occasional examples, particularly in the cruise sector, where sexual harassment has been dealt with more comprehensively.

Union representatives had a number of practical suggestions to improve the retention of women seafarers on board ships. They include:

- allowing women flexible working patterns in order to combine their role aboard with their domestic role ashore;

- providing childcare facilities to enable them to participate fully in company and trade union activities;

- providing condoms and oral contraceptives (the Pill) aboard;

- developing an ILO policy in relation to gender and seafarers in order to support the efforts of individual trade unions in lobbying for women's issues.

The International Transport Workers' Federation

Worldwide there are more that 590 transport trade unions, many of which represent seafarers. In 1886, the International Transport Workers' Federation (ITF) was founded in London by seafarers' and dockers' union leaders. Today, the federation consists of affiliated trade unions from 136 countries and represents approximately 5 million workers. It defines its role as supporting members and finding ways of defending "the interests of transport workers in the global economy". In doing so, it seeks to bring unions together, enabling them to share information and develop common strategies, and it has set up a number of specialist working groups to deal with more specialized areas of interest. It represents the voice of labour in the ILO and participates in IMO meetings through the International Confederation of Free Trade Unions (ICFTU), in which it has a consultative status. As such, it has an important role to play in promoting and developing seafarers' rights, including those of its women members.

In 1994, the ITF recognized the need to address specific issues concerning women seafarers and by 1998 it had established a Women's Committee. Composed of 30 members and including both industrial and regional representatives, its role is to advise the ITF's Executive Board on gender-related matters.

The ITF has an anti-discriminatory policy, introduced in 1999, which aims to address harassment and discrimination. As one ITF official explained:

> What we have done in the maritime sector is probably focused around one thing, an anti-harassment and discrimination policy that covers race and gender, which we have printed and distributed and supplied to our network of inspectors. And we have also run courses for our inspectors on questions relating to harassment and discrimination.

In addition, the ITF seeks to discourage the differential pay of men and women and members of different ethnic groups and has sought to reach agreements with employers relating to issues such as pregnancy and maternity benefits, as exemplified by the signing of the IMEC model agreement.

Despite these new efforts to address gender-related areas of policy, ITF representatives acknowledge that within the trade union movement there is a certain level of resistance to prioritizing gender-related issues and consequently these issues are not very high on the agenda of many member unions.

MET institutions

Seventeen MET institutions from various parts of the world participated in this study. More than half these institutions are located in OECD countries, with the rest based in developing countries in other world regions (Eastern Europe, Latin America and Africa, and southern Asia). They represent 6,518 students currently being trained for employment at sea, of whom 647 (10 per cent) are women.

Policy

Women are reported to be receiving training in all world regions except for parts of southern Asia. They are not concentrated in any particular region. Only four of the 17 institutions reported having an equal opportunities policy relating to the recruitment of women. In some cases, MET institutions have little control over the gender composition of the enrolment as their governments prohibit the recruitment of women to nautical courses. For example, a large country in Asia with a large labour supply has 31 MET institutions, none of which is able to recruit female students because of central government regulation. In other cases, however, the immediate constraints come from shipowners and managers. In most European countries, cadets are recruited and then sponsored directly by shipowners. A senior staff member in a European college explained:

> Yes, it [the recruitment] is purely down to the companies. We have nothing to do with their sea time at all. [Individual students] They can't apply to the college. The companies take them on in the first place and decide which college they are going to. [...] The companies decide where the students are going to go during their sea time.

Despite these constraints on recruitment, there are, nevertheless, a number of regions where the recruitment of women trainee seafarers is increasing. Some nautical schools are playing a more active role in the enrolment of women students. Since 2000, the SMU in China has allowed women to take part in its navigational training programme, while at the FNB in Spain a special programme promoting the enrolment of women in technical courses has resulted in a fivefold increase in the representation of female students in the faculty. As a result, 25 per cent of the student population in its nautical school is now female, compared with only 5 per cent in 1996. There are similar cases in other world regions.

As the recruitment of male students becomes increasingly difficult, supply-side pressure may account for the rise in the intake of female trainees in certain regions. For several decades, "overcapacity" has haunted MET institutions in OECD countries. As one European senior examiner noted:

> Not many trainees, this is the problem. Schools have already closed down – there are just too many schools. Maybe one school is enough, which is a national question. The MET institution therefore has to turn to women for a new source of enrolment.

This problem of overcapacity also affects MET institutions in some developing countries, to which some have also responded by increasing their female intake. Interestingly, some of these institutions report that their female graduates are more "marketable" than their male counterparts. Although these cases have only been reported in the Far East, it is possible that they reflect a similar pattern across the world.

"Appropriate" courses for women

In many MET institutions, both navigation and engineering courses are, in theory, open to women. In practice, however, most women students enrol on navigation courses. Among the MET institutions contacted, 97 per cent of the women students were being trained as deck officers and only 3 per cent as engineers. When asked about this discrepancy in their intakes, teaching staff often referred to working conditions in engine rooms (dirty, hot, with limited space and greater demand for physical strength and hands-on skill, and so on), which were considered to be unattractive to, and unsuitable for, women. Two typical comments were:

> The practical engineering side – it's very much hands on at sea. It can be a very dirty, hot, lousy job.

> Maritime engineering is not a proper subject for women. As engineers, you have to work down below in the engine room, where it is hot and dirty and women are more likely to get sexually abused.

In offering courses to women students, some institutions take a somewhat pragmatic approach and require that women undertake additional modules designed primarily to provide training for shore-based jobs. As one respondent explained:

We genuinely hope that these girls can get jobs on ships. But we know it may not be easy for them to get employed, and we must be responsible for their future. That's why we also offer them so many modules for land-based jobs. We will try our best to help them get jobs on board ships – we genuinely want them to be successful seafarers. But we have to prepare for otherwise, to ensure these girls will get some maritime-related jobs when they finish their studies.

In doing so, institutions may be said to be discriminating against women since these compulsory courses for women are twice as expensive as normal maritime training fees, thereby effectively excluding some potential female students.

Performance

Women students were widely reported to perform at least as well as male students, both technically and academically. As two lecturers noted:

Their ability is equal to and, say, sometimes better than boys. You get good and bad in all cases, but I think they're no problem at all. Some of the best cadets are women at the moment.

I keep an eye on the reports of all cadets in general and they don't seem any worse; in fact, they tend to be a little bit better than the male cadets.

There were reports of women consistently outperforming men, which was attributed to a greater determination and commitment on their part to prove themselves in an overwhelmingly male domain.

Historically, it's a job only for men, and the women who go into this industry must be exceptionally good. They must say every time, "I'm better than the men".

Some institutions in Europe also noted lower drop-out rates among female students. Once again, this was attributed to the greater determination on the part of women to succeed in this industry.

Women within MET institutions

Despite the greater presence of women students in some MET institutions, none of the colleges contacted have gender issues incorporated into their core curricula. There is a belief that potential problems on board ship should not be anticipated, and in one respondent's words, "Students should not be taught about the problem before the problem appears." In a small number of cases, staff expressed their own confusion about having women cadets/students in nautical schools. One said: "I honestly don't understand why they should decide to do this at all." To some, the very idea of women seafarers represents the antithesis of the traditional image of women as wives and mothers, and they have reservations about accepting women on their courses. Nevertheless, in most cases, lecturers appear to regard women students as unproblematic and indeed welcome their participation.

Prospects in the labour market

In European countries, many students are sponsored by shipping companies, or supported jointly with grants from their governments and contributions from their future employers. In these cases, women, as well as men, do not seem to have much difficulty in finding jobs when they finish their studies. Nevertheless, institutions in Europe have different expectations regarding future job opportunities for their women students. Lecturers in other world regions also identified uncertainties over employment prospects. One told us:

> It's hard to say at the moment. We'll have to see in two years' time. At the moment, our graduates are extremely popular with employers. Each graduate can be sought after by five employers. But all our graduates now are men. It's hard to predict the situation for these girls. We have done an employer survey and learned that they would consider employing some girls for their land-based positions. Honestly, we are not sure if they will welcome these girls to work on their ships. That's why we are a bit cautious and do not want to take too much risk, and we offer them extra-curriculum courses. We're not sure …

The future enrolment of women

Many MET institutions were not enthusiastic about further promoting their courses to women students. In their view, the industry's top priority should be to improve overall conditions of work in order to make a seafaring career more attractive to all seafarers, regardless of gender. However, some institutions suggested that the following steps should be taken to attract more women seafarers:

- The image of the industry should be improved and national and inter-national awareness of the maritime industry should be increased. Such awareness-raising programmes should include a gender-related element, emphasizing the suitability of seafaring as a career for women.

- Shipping companies should support MET institutions by offering work placements and post-qualifying employment to women.

- Government regulations prohibiting women from enrolling at MET institutions should be revised to allow for the recruitment of women students.

Summary

This chapter reported on the policies and practices of international organizations, governments, employers, trade unions and MET institutions. In doing so, it has highlighted the extent to which these various maritime bodies are addressing the issue of gender. The evidence suggests that there is considerable variation in the approach taken by shipowners and ship managers to issues relating to the employment of women. Less diversity is apparent in the approaches of international organizations, governments, trade unions and MET institutions. Such groups have tended to develop comprehensive policy statements but in general have yet to refine these in order to address specific gender-related issues in more detail.

The IMO strategy for integrating women into the shipping industry started in 1988 with the designation of a Focal Point for WID, and has been followed by two four-year recruitment and sensitization programmes. The organization's strategy has mostly focused on the need to increase the participation rate of women in the maritime sector and has not been addressed specifically to women seafarers. Despite this, it recognizes that less than 2 per cent of the seafaring workforce is composed of women, and stresses the fact that technical improvements in shipboard operations have allowed for an increase in the number of women employed in the maritime sector.

The ILO's Discrimination (Employment and Occupation) Convention, 1958 (No. 111), establishes the fundamental principle and right to non-discrimination on the grounds of sex, including in the maritime industry. The ILO's Declaration of Fundamental Principles and Rights and its Follow-Up in 1998 reaffirmed this principle and right to non-discrimination. In 1999 the Director-General of the ILO issued a policy statement highlighting its commitment to gender equality and gender mainstreaming.

National governments, on the other hand, have not shown any proactive policy in respect to women seafarers. In OECD countries, they tend to comply with generic government policies, ensuring that policies relating to women at work are applied to women seafarers.

Shipping companies in general do not have specific policies relating to women seafarers. There are no policies against their employment, but in some countries shipowners can tend to be very negative regarding employing women at sea. This is more evident with shipowners that have never employed female staff before. In some cases, distinctions are made between what is considered appropriate for women seafarers, with some shipowners indicating a few posts where they would never employ women, such as bosun or chief engineer. However, shipowners used to employing women at sea, irrespective of the positions they hold, have, in general, no complaints. Indeed, many of them highlighted the fact that women seafarers can be extremely hard workers.

Most cruise companies have sexual harassment policies, although they are not specifically designed to address women seafarers. In most cases, cargo companies have no such policies in place. Pregnancy and maternity leave are, in general, non-existent.

Employers' organizations have not addressed women seafarers' issues specifically, leaving them to individual members. However, some information can still be found in the ISF's *Guidelines on good employment practice* and in the IMEC model agreement, regarding maternity.

Most trade unions do not have equal opportunities policies or any policy specifically relating to women. However, some reported the existence of well-defined policies on women seafarers and effective infrastructures for dealing with gender issues. In 1998, the ITF established a Women's Committee to advise its Executive Board on gender-related matters. The ITF also has an anti-discriminatory policy, which was introduced in 1999.

MET institutions also do not have specific policies for women in place; nor have they incorporated issues regarding women into their curricula. As the MET institutions that participated in the survey reveal, women are being trained in all world regions with the exception of parts of southern Asia, although this may soon change, in India at least (*Fairplay*, 2002). Finally, most MET staff seemed satisfied with the performance of their female students.

POLICIES IN PRACTICE: THE EXPERIENCES OF WOMEN SEAFARERS

5

Having considered the policies and practices relating to women seafarers from the standpoint of shipowners and ship managers, it is important to examine the actual experiences of women working on board ship in order to identify how these policies translate into action. Drawing on the accounts of women seafarers working in the cruise and commercial sectors of the shipping industry, as both marine and hotel/catering personnel, this chapter explores the issues that have an impact on women and their work, and the effect that these issues have on their careers. The effectiveness and adequacy of the industry's current approach to gender issues is considered in conjunction with ways of further improving conditions for women working at sea.

Early experiences

Reasons for choosing a seafaring career

There is some evidence to suggest that both men and women choose seafaring as a career having learned and become enthusiastic about it as a result of talking with seafaring family members or friends (Lane, 1986; Zhao, 1999). The data collected for this study lend some support to these findings, particularly in areas with a strong seafaring tradition such as Germany, the Philippines, Sweden and the United Kingdom. Typically, women seafarers referred to the sea as being a part of their life and local culture, as the following extracts illustrate:

> I must have been about 16, I suppose. My dad was in the Royal Navy. I was brought up in [a coastal area], so the sea was sort of part of my life really. And I wanted to go to the Royal Navy to begin with, but didn't get in [...] so [I] went to the merchant navy and got a place at [name of college].

My father's at sea, my uncle's at sea, my grandfathers were at sea. I'm from [name of area], where there's a really strong seafaring tradition, and a lot of my friends came here [MET institution].

However, not all the women had seafarers in their families and in one area of south-east Asia none of the women interviewed reported having seafaring relatives. Their reasons for going to sea are more diverse and include wanting to see the world, wanting to "escape" from their families, enjoying engineering and simply making a "spur of the moment" decision:

You just want to be away from your family, away from the chains of your family. My mum was a very difficult woman to live with. So my first thought of joining was that I would be away from my family.

I have no idea – because I'm not interested in office jobs, I'm not interested in admin. work and all that. So I decided to do engineering.

In the cruise sector, women from developing countries often cited potential earnings and the opportunity to save money as the most significant motivating factor for working at sea. The economic situation in their home countries, high inflation and poor job opportunities, along with the financial needs of their families, led these women to seek employment on cruise ships, where they could earn higher salaries in "hard currency". Women from Eastern Europe were also attracted to the industry by the chance to travel and meet people from different countries and cultures. However, most Asian women appeared to focus almost exclusively on the financial advantages of a career at sea.

In contrast to women from developing countries, women from developed countries seem less motivated by finance. Indeed, although they are generally employed in higher ranks, some reported earning wages that were markedly lower than what they would expect to earn in shore-based jobs. For these women, the main attraction of the cruise sector is primarily the opportunity to travel and "see the world for free". A small number of women from these countries have at least one seafaring parent or relative and they feel this inspired them to take up a sea career. The distinction between the motivation of women in developed countries and those from developing countries is highlighted by our data on cruise vessels: 69 per cent of women from developing countries reported that their main reason to go to sea was to earn more money, compared with 32 per cent from developed countries. Of the former, 27 per cent cited their main reason as being "to see other countries", compared with 48 per cent in the latter group.

Family support

Whatever their motivation for joining, many women in the marine department have to overcome family resistance to or reservations about their decision to pursue a career at sea. Some parents are shocked that their daughters want to go to sea, while others are afraid of the dangers that such a career choice might entail. The following examples of parental response were given:

Initially, my parents freaked out. They were not happy, because no one in our family had been to sea before. My mum was typically Asian, thinking of the mind of the seafarer. The only thing that seamen do: drugs, womanize, alcohol. So she was not too comfortable with it, though she was supportive. My dad was not supportive at all initially.

She [my Mum] thinks it is very dangerous because I work on tankers and the thing is, I'm alone in a world of men.

Not all women seafarers reported reservations from their families, however, and among those who faced initial resistance, some subsequently found that their parents were supportive later in their careers and were even disappointed when they chose to leave the sea. One said:

It took me a year to convince my parents that this was what I wanted to do. When I told them I was quitting, they were actually quite disappointed.

The level of family support varies among women in the hotel and catering sector of the industry. Some reported that their parents were proud of their career choice, inspired, perhaps, by images of the industry as glamorous and exciting. For others, the prospect of a long period of separation is a cause for concern. Unlike women working in the marine department in the commercial sector, none of the women in the cruise sector reported that their families were worried about the dangers associated with life at sea. A number of women from developing countries who are parents and who have no partners or have partners who are also seafarers can only continue their career at sea because their extended family on shore is able to provide childcare.

Access to maritime education and professional training

In the marine sector, some older women seafarers described how, in the past, they had been prevented from joining particular courses. Today, however, gaining access to institutions providing maritime education no longer appears to be such a problem for women and indeed seems to be encouraged in countries such as Germany, Ghana and Singapore. However, gaining access to an institution is only part of the picture; once inside an MET institution, women reported encountering a certain degree of prejudice and hostility from some lecturers and staff members. Two women described their experiences:

> There's one lecturer who definitely does not believe that women should be at sea full stop. … But there are others that think it's slightly unusual. There are some who, whenever I walk into a lecture, are a bit surprised to see me, despite the fact that I've been there a year. It's a shock for them that women are now at sea. Things like that. Most of them are all right now, though.

> Initially, there were some Malay marine lecturers who said: "You shouldn't join [name of course] because it's quite unsuitable for women. You should join [name of different course], which gives you a choice of going out to sea or working in an office." But when I was 18 and people said that kind of thing to me, I always said: "You think I can't do it? Well, I'm going to prove to you that I can."

In one focus group, female cadets offered an explanation for the attitudes of some of their male lecturers:

> You accept that most of the lecturers left sea before women really started going to sea. They don't know what it's like for us.

Cadets also reported difficulties in finding cadet or apprentice placements on vessels. Occasionally, such reports were corroborated by companies and individuals directly involved in the supervision and administration of seafarer training. The problems all appear to stem from a reluctance on the part of many companies to employ or train women seafarers. Despite the best efforts of MET institutions, some women graduates are forced to defer their career development and remain in shore jobs. One woman explained:

> I wanted to go to sea. The thing is there is only one company in Singapore that will accept women. And it chose two out of the four of us who wanted to go to sea. So the other girl and I stayed on shore and we do repair jobs for some small companies. [...] They tried to [arrange sea time as a cadet], but couldn't.

Most women working in the industry's hotel sector gain their maritime training through their first employers and on board their first vessels, rather than through MET institutions. Women find jobs with cruise companies through advertisements or by word of mouth, and are often recruited by crewing agencies, both in developed and developing countries. Some women from developed countries reported having no face-to-face interviews and were recruited on the basis of their written application and a photograph.

The reported time from being accepted at interview to being placed on a ship varies from three weeks to several months. In some countries, age limits are set on applicants and these differ for male and female applicants. For some agents in the Philippines, for example, the age limit for men to be employed on cruise ships is 40, while for women it is 29. Access to the industry is also often constrained by women being unable to pay for a visa, medical examination and their airfare to join the vessel, which together can cost more than US$1,000.

Although women working in the hotel and catering sector of cruise shipping typically have little experience of the industry prior to joining their first vessel, very few women reported receiving any comprehensive training or induction before embarking. Induction training can include information about life aboard, employers' expectations as well as training on company policies. Information on company policies and advice and guidance about issues such as sexual harassment are often conveyed during initial interviews with the crewing agent or cruise company, through information sheets or booklets, or take place during on-board safety meetings after employment has begun. Providing training in the form of written information is not always very effective, however. Some women reported never having read their booklets: staff typically work a 12-hour day and sleep an average five hours a night, and consequently they prefer to catch up on sleep in their free time to reading booklets on company policy. However, when given, pre-boarding training is viewed very positively by women and also appears to have a beneficial effect on their experience aboard ship. Most women reported receiving safety training, either prior to joining the vessel or immediately after embarkation.

Working aboard ship

Acceptance on board

It seems that there is still considerable resistance among companies to the employment of women. In one Western European country, where women have been present in the industry for a significant period of time, one official estimated that only 30 per cent of companies offering apprentices places on board their vessels would accept women. The following is a typical comment on the difficulties women occasionally have in obtaining work or training placements on board ship:

> I think it is a little bit more difficult for me [...] and for other women to find a job. [...] I think maybe the companies think, "Ah, maybe we'll get a man. Let's have a look. OK, you send us your application, but maybe we will look around." And if there's nobody, they will call me back.

After long periods of comprehensive training, some women are made to do jobs that bear no relevance to their training and professional development:

> At first, four of us girls were placed on passenger ships as waitresses. I was not happy, because I had invested so many years learning engineering. I asked to change my post on the ship and told the captain and the political commissar that I wanted to work in the engine room. They warned me that it would be very hot and uncomfortable in that part of the ship. But I insisted. They eventually gave in and moved me to the engine room.

Just as there is opposition to the employment of women from shore-side staff, so too are women confronted with a certain level of resistance from their male shipboard colleagues. Such confrontations take a variety of forms, ranging from overt and vociferous hostility to prejudiced comments in the guise of "humour". The intention of such behaviour seems to be to get the message across that the ship is not an appropriate workplace for women. One woman said:

> Within the first ten days of being aboard my first ship, the mate told me that he didn't think that women should be at sea and that we weren't suited to being at sea and we all argue with each other. And he just gave me the cleaning jobs the whole time; I was cleaning internal stairwells for three months. And the captain didn't agree with women working at sea either.

Another female seafarer described the way in which humour was used on one ship to make her feel uncomfortable:

> I received a lot of "women should be in the kitchen" type of jokes and blonde hair jokes.

It seems that, especially during their first few months on board a vessel, or early in their careers, women encounter a number of men who find it difficult to accept that they can be suitably qualified and willing and capable of carrying out seafaring work. There are indications that this is a particular problem for women engineers working in hot, dirty conditions, regarded as the very antithesis of a feminine environment:

> I get a lot of: "Why does a woman want to become an engineer? It's a filthy dirty job. Why does a woman want to do that? She doesn't want to get dirt under her nails." There was surprise and bafflement. They could not see why a woman would want to do a job that was dirty, smelly, hot, sweaty. They couldn't see how a woman would want to do that.

During their first months on board, women reported having to accept higher levels of surveillance prior to becoming "accepted" and, on a number of occasions, of being "tested" by their colleagues and superiors to see if they were made of the "right stuff" for the job:

> I was cleaning bilges [the lowest internal portion of the hull] out. I was on my hands and knees, covered from head to toe in, no other way to describe it, but shit. The other cadet was typing stuff on home computers, standing on the bridge while I spent eight months painting, chipping, greasing, cleaning. The lads I was sailing with spent about four months doing those awful jobs and then they were up on the bridge in a clean environment. They will push you [a woman] a lot, lot harder.

> Some men do take it out on you a lot. They really do not like it and therefore they treat you badly to try and put you off.

However, over time it seems that most women, with a great deal of effort on their part, are able to overcome the reservations of their male colleagues. One female engineer who had received comments such as "You shouldn't be here", "You should be a model instead", "You don't have the body to work in an engine room" reported that "when you do the same things as they do, after a time it's OK". This view was shared by most of the women respondents.

Hostility is not the only form in which male prejudices manifest themselves. Some men were described as being "over-protective" and paternalistic. This could be a source of frustration to women seeking to prove themselves in a male-dominated environment. As one woman explained:

> There are generally two types of guys. One type expects more because they say, "Women can't work on board". And if you make one mistake, they say, "OK, I knew it, I knew it. Now you see, she's not capable." And then there is the other type. If you do something absolutely normal, like hammer in a nail [...], they say, "Oh, my God, great. You can do it. I knew it. Fantastic."

Women in senior positions reported additional, though infrequent, problems with men who seemed unable to take orders from women in authority. One explained:

> A lot of men have problems taking orders from a female. The frustration didn't come when I was a cadet, because I didn't really deal with the crew so much. But when you become an officer, that is when the frustration starts.

Such problems can also extend to women's dealings with shore-side personnel, such as pilots, stevedores and customs officials, many of whom have little experience of dealing with women in senior positions on board ship or indeed ashore. One experienced female captain described how:

I was master and we were leaving Hong Kong and I had the pilot on board. [...] He came to the bridge and the chief engineer said, "This is the pilot, this is the master" [and he said], "No, it's not possible. A woman can't be a master", and the chief mate was speechless, looking to the pilot, looking to me. I was speechless. Then I said, "Maybe it's the first time you've seen a female captain, but I'm the captain and we should sail the ship from this port." "No, it's not possible. I'll call the traffic control." So he called the traffic control and said, "There's a young lady and she says she's the master. But I've never seen a female master, so what shall I do? Shall I disembark?"

Women seafarers in the hotel and catering sector of the industry appear to be more readily accepted by their male colleagues than those working in the marine department. This is probably due to the fact that the work women do in this sector often more closely reflects the types of jobs that are traditionally considered "women's work", for example, cleaning, shop work and employment in the beauty industry. Women working in the food and beverage sector, such as waitresses, reported some reluctance on the part of their male colleagues to accept them, since some of the tasks involved in their work, such as carrying trays of crockery and tableware, can be physically strenuous. Such a lack of acceptance typically manifests itself in offers of assistance and attempts to prevent women carrying heavy loads. As with women in the commercial sector, women working in these environments often feel that they have to prove themselves in order to be accepted by their male colleagues:

Sometimes they help us, you know. Because they say, "Oh, no, no. Don't worry, you know, you can do it." I say, "Come on, I can do it. I am strong enough to do it, so let me do it." They say, "OK, OK. But be careful you know, don't kill yourself." "It's OK, no problem." I do it, you know. I do it, I don't have any problems, you know. It's a little bit heavy but I can do it, no problem.

Equal opportunities and promotion

Many women officers find that, once they have become established in a career at sea, their companies are prepared to offer them the same career options as their male colleagues. Occasionally, some even suggested that their promotion prospects might be enhanced as a result of their gender:

Because there are so few women at sea, companies see that promoting a woman is good for publicity. They can brag about how many women they have at sea. [...] Also, I think they think that if they don't promote her quickly enough, then she could say, "Well, that's sexist. You're discriminating against me because I am a woman." So, if anything, I think it [promotion] may be a little bit quicker, so that they don't get seen as being sexist and they get seen in a good light because they've got women at sea in positions of rank.

The fact that many women officers do not feel discriminated against in terms of promotion possibly reflects a situation whereby companies that have an equal opportunities approach to recruitment also promote officers on the basis of merit, not sex. However, given that many companies are still unwilling to recruit women seafarers in the first place, women who need to change company in order to be promoted (as a result of limited vacancies in their current company) have, in effect, fewer opportunities than men, which inevitably restricts their prospects for promotion.

Nevertheless, some women do feel that they are denied opportunities that are available to their male colleagues because of their sex:

> I think actually that half the time the company does not offer much. I heard one of the superiors from the company saying that no matter how good you [a woman] are, they will not make you chief engineer.

There is some evidence that such discrimination deters women from remaining in a sea-based career. The woman quoted above explained that, when considering her future, this weighed quite heavily on her mind. Despite her original ambition to become a chief engineer, she ended her sea career and sought a shore position. She explained:

> I was very disappointed. [...] I thought more about it. "Should I waste my time with the company if it's not willing to promote women or to assist me in my career?"

Some women in the hotel and catering sector believe that they will not be promoted to senior ranks:

> Women have no chance of getting promoted on this ship. The hotel manager is a man, all the supervisors are men. They are older than we are. Even then, there is little hope of getting promoted.

A small number of women in this sector also suggested that promotion opportunities could be linked to ethnicity and to the granting of sexual favours. This latter issue is discussed in the section in this chapter on sexual harassment.

Social relationships

Many of the women in the marine department who took part in the survey described sailing alone aboard ship in male to female ratios of up to 30:1. Such ratios are generally not found in the hotel sector of the industry, where ratios vary but women constitute approximately 20 per cent of the workforce. Inevitably, being part of a minority group in a male-dominated environment raises social as well as work-related issues.

On board cargo ships, social interaction with the outside world is limited and life can be very monotonous. In this setting, seafarers resort, in large part, to the use of humour as a way of "oiling the wheels" of social contact. Often such humour focuses on both real and imaginary women and can be interpreted as highly sexist, sexualized and derogatory. On board ship, women not only have to handle such generalized "jokes", but they frequently become targets of similar remarks and so-called "practical jokes". In many cases, the expectation is that they should put up with, and even pretend to be amused by, such behaviour, which would be quite unimaginable and almost certainly not tolerated by anyone in land-based work settings:

> Things were going missing from my cabin, including my underwear. [...] I caught the crew on video and I showed the Old Man. But because he thought it was a good ruse, he didn't report it to the company.

The impact of the use of such humour can be compounded by the tendency for women to be an almost obsessive target of gossip. This can have a major effect on women's behaviour on board and can cause them considerable unease and social discomfort. A number of women discussed this issue during the survey's interviews. The following extracts from their transcripts are illustrative:

> They make up a lot of stories and it's upsetting when you hear stories like that.

> If you find somebody who you can chat with and somebody sees, they won't be happy. So rumours start flying and people say, "Oh, she's in love with this fella. They're having an affair", and all that kind of stuff.

> If I whisper, they think I'm making love. So I learned to speak very loudly, you know. I speak loudly to everyone. It became part of me – this very high frequency. You can hear my voice from the galley!

Unlike inappropriate expressions of "humour", which do not seem to trouble women on board cruise ships, gossip is a major cause of concern for women in both the cruise and commercial sectors. One respondent described the ways in which people question the most innocent of activities:

> If they see you entering anyone's cabin, they think, "Who's having sex?", even if you are just talking or watching television.

These kinds of comments, remarks and jokes, and consequent slurs on women and their reputations, make many women modify their behaviour on board quite dramatically. In the marine department of the industry, where women frequently work alone in otherwise all-male environments, many women spend excessive amounts of time in their cabins pursuing solitary activities. One woman described how she tried to avoid gossip by minimizing her contact with others on board, at first avoiding talking to other people altogether:

> Initially, I was quite upset about it [the gossip]. So for quite some time I tried not to talk to anybody: "Hello", "Hello", that's it, finished. Then I find that even when I do that, the rumours still fly, so I told myself it doesn't matter. Whatever they want to say, they can say. As long as I didn't do anything wrong, I'm not afraid of them. So I just carry on and try not to be too friendly. I just have a short chat and that's it. So most of the time I keep to myself.

Another described how she was excluded from the common practice of seafarers socializing in cabins in small groups:

> You can't just go to somebody's room and sit down, because everybody, all the crew, are men. I was the only woman. And I was a captain, so you can imagine how miserable it was – very miserable.

Managing a balance between integrating with the crew and being considered aloof is something that many women find especially difficult on board ship. As one woman explained:

> There's a very fine line between being a good-time girl and being an ice maiden. And it's extremely thin. If you sit in the cabin all the time, then nobody likes you. If you're in the bar too much, then it's, "Oh, she's in the bar too much". It's really difficult to decide what to do.

Women in the cruise sector also tend to limit their interaction with male crew members to protect themselves from gossip. However, the consequences of withdrawing are perhaps less severe than for women working in the cargo sector, since the higher numbers of women aboard mean that women can remove themselves from male domains without socially isolating themselves completely.

Social isolation also extends to periods of shore leave when, for a variety of reasons, male colleagues do not necessarily invite their female colleagues to join them:

> You feel excluded when you get to the port. I had a colleague who, when he was going ashore, would invite me – he was younger than me. But none of my other colleagues invited me – none of the men would invite us to go ashore.

Sexual harassment

Defining sexual harassment is a complex task and it is not our intention to offer a comprehensive definition here (for a full definition of sexual harassment, see Appendix XIII). Nevertheless, it is the case that in organizations where people work together in clear occupational hierarchies and some individuals occupy positions of power and authority over others, there exists a potential for individuals to abuse their powers in the interests of their own sexual gratification and to the detriment of their subordinates. On board ship, such occupational hierarchies are both ubiquitous and rigidly observed, and seafarers themselves are very conscious of the impact their senior officers can have on their shipboard lives and indeed on their entire seafaring careers. Such awareness of the importance of maintaining good relationships with senior officers is illustrated by the following comment:

> When you sail with officers, there are senior officers who have to write a report on you. If you don't have a good rapport with them, then your promotion is gone.

It is in such environments that junior personnel in any organization are most vulnerable to sexual harassment and exploitation. A raft of examples was given to SIRC researchers from women in both the marine and hotel sectors of the industry and the following are illustrative of the range and kinds of points raised:

> I heard somebody telling me after I signed off from that ship that there are a couple of holes in the toilet. I tried to check for holes when I first joined the ship, but I didn't find any. Anyway, there are peepholes and they can peep at you when you take a shower.

> Most people try to take [sexual] advantage of you if you're a cadet, because you can't pull rank on them.

> There was some problem with the chief officer. He was from Poland and he had been on the vessel for one year at the time. And he couldn't understand that I wanted to be alone during the night and one evening I had to punch him to get him out of my room.

> He was the bar manager. He put pressure on me to go to his cabin. He was my boss, you know. And he give me a hard time because I didn't want to stay with him.

In many cultures, socio-sexual interaction is initiated by men, who may, therefore, see such behaviour as acceptable and "normal". Problems aboard ship arise both when superordinates make advances to subordinates, perhaps without appreciating the pressure that this places on them, and when colleagues behave inappropriately, that is, when their advances are unwanted and their behaviour is offensive or threatening. These problems can be exacerbated by the context of shipboard life where people are confined and unable to leave settings in which they are uncomfortable and are, in addition, unable to gain access to external sources of support. As one woman starkly commented:

> I am alone in a world of men, so anything can happen out at sea, where I cannot shout for help.

The impact of sexual harassment of any form on women on board ship can be considerable and can have a direct impact on their work as well as on their personal well-being. One woman described a series of incidents that occurred when she was a young cadet:

> When I got up at quarter to 12, to go up to the bridge to work, he was lying down on his side – you could see him from my door – totally naked and he was masturbating, holding a magazine. So my natural instinct was that he was drunk. So I just walked off. But it kept on happening, on and off, for about two or three days. So it really freaked me out when one day he turned his head and smiled at me. So I kind of got scared. I started coming up late for my watches and I asked my senior to come down to pick me up.

Women cope with harassment on board in a number of ways. Often they withdraw from social situations, perhaps choosing to avoid going to parties and general on-board events or choosing to leave such occasions early.

> When you go to a barbecue party, for example, and you sit there and drink a beer and eat something, and you feel that some of them are drinking too much, then I try to go back to my cabin and just leave it all behind.

Some women resort to locking themselves in their cabins for security at night. One woman described how she learned the "hard way" to lock herself in every evening. Having woken up to find a crew member molesting her in her bed one night, she stopped leaving her cabin door unlocked and became extremely concerned with her safety:

> I now know that I must lock my door before I go to sleep and I check it at least three times. And it's awful to think that you have to lock yourself away, but it's a fact of life.

Some women take drastic means to avoid being harassed, altering and "de-feminizing" their appearance. One woman engineer described how she shaved her head on board in order to appear as "unattractive" to her male colleagues as possible. She explained:

> If I don't look too feminine and don't act too femininely, I should be OK. And that's the mentality I have.

As these examples illustrate, women on board ship are prepared to go to some considerable and arguably unacceptable lengths to avoid being harassed by male colleagues. Inappropriate male behaviour is often, therefore, left unchallenged and unmodified and may, as a result, be frequently repeated. Companies could play a role in highlighting the unacceptability of some male behaviour by introducing policies on sexual harassment and by supporting women when incidents are brought to their attention. Ashore, company policies on sexual harassment are increasingly common, but on board cargo ships they are virtually unheard of. In the cruise sector, policies on sexual harassment are more likely to exist. Some larger employers were reported to have strong policies in place which emphasize the lack of tolerance of any form of sexual harassment.

However, not all women staff are aware of their company's policy on sexual harassment. Policies appear to be most effective where efforts have been made to convey company policy to employees through company training and induction courses. Such training is often done prior to new staff joining a vessel and usually includes illustrations of unacceptable behaviour and details of company disciplinary procedures. Employees tend to be very positive about the existence and high profile of such policies, feeling that they reduce incidences of sexual harassment and create a more comfortable working environment:

> On [ship name], we had very good safety. I felt confident there about the sexual harassment issue. We had a very good safety meeting and a safety manager told us to go to him and tell him or his security guys if we heard anything wrong.

However, for many women, the strategies disseminating company policy are ineffective. Some employees are given booklets to read, while others are informed of company policy during initial interviews with the company or recruiting agent. The issue is also covered during on-board safety meetings. Some women reported that company policy documentation was available via senior staff. There are, however, women who receive no training on company policy and who are vague about their company's stance on sexual harassment and on a number of other important issues relating to their employment and well-being. This lack of awareness of company policy is reiterated in our survey data of women seafarers in the cruise sector. Here, women working for the same company, and indeed on the same ship, reported notably different understandings of company policy on sexual harassment.

Our interview data suggest that the simple existence of a company policy is insufficient: to be effective a policy needs to be actively disseminated, with the company showing clear support for it through positive action. The prevalence of sexual harassment was reported very differently in our two sets of data. Nearly all the women in the in-depth face-to-face interviews reported experiencing some form of sexual harassment, but only one in five of the women completing the questionnaires on cruise ships reported having experienced harassment. Since the in-depth interviews included women working in the cruise sector, we can attribute these differences in prevalence to methodological differences: face-to-face interviews are a more sensitive instrument for eliciting and reporting such matters. It should also be noted that many women also reported experiences of harassment of a non-sexual kind, particularly aggressive and abusive behaviour from superiors.

When policies are ineffective in preventing sexual harassment, they also appear to be inefficient when it comes to making staff feel confident enough to make a formal complaint. In the cruise sector, several economically vulnerable women in lower ranks and from developing countries felt wary of making a complaint for fear it would lead to them losing their jobs. This was particularly true for those whose experience had not been witnessed by other employees and would, therefore, be a case of "their word against someone else's".

Formal complaints are often only made in situations in which women believe in the commitment of their employers to eliminate sexual harassment and/or where they have a witness who is willing to support their testimony. On the occasions that women sought company help, or the support of senior officers, responses varied. Occasionally, companies and senior managers took action to address inappropriate behaviour, sometimes removing the "offenders" from ships, but more generally their response was less helpful. One woman reported being prevented from joining a vessel because a woman aboard that ship, from the same country, had previously made a complaint about sexual harassment, and as a result the ship would no longer have women of that nationality aboard. On another vessel, the head of security – the point of call for complaints on sexual harassment – was himself a perpetrator of sexual harassment. Often, therefore, women feel "punished" for having brought harassment to the attention of others:

> He tried something funny and initially I was afraid to tell anybody, even though I was quite OK with the other officers. It's just that you are afraid that if you were to say something, they might not believe you. So when the thing finally came out in the open, I was surprised that the company took me off the ship, instead of him. And then when I asked for an explanation, they told me that it would be easier to get a replacement for me, because I'm a cadet, rather than a replacement for him, because he's on the management side.

> As soon as I saw my personnel manager, I told him, and he said I should expect that sort of thing because I was at sea and I should deal with it myself.

When complaints are addressed effectively, women appear to be more con-fident of both their right to complain and the likelihood that the complaint will be taken seriously. It also appears to have a positive effect on the crew as a whole.

Menstruation

Many modern ships operate with minimum crewing levels and in and out of 24-hour working ports. As a result, seafarers find their opportunities for shore leave increasingly curtailed and in many cases non-existent. Senior officers may never have the opportunity to take shore leave as their responsibilities to their ship and company require them to remain on board even while berthed. In this context, and given that there is increasing international regulation concerning waste disposal at sea, women find that dealing with menstruation is becoming more and more of a problem. On most cargo ships there are no facilities for either the purchase or disposal of sanitary materials. This issue is frequently overlooked by male seafarers and shore-side staff, although it is one which can cause women considerable anxiety and humiliation as well as friction between men and women on board:

> Sometimes, when you run out of sanitary pads on board, and you can't go ashore, you can't tell your chief officer that "I'm trying to get sanitary pads – that's why I want to go out". He normally sees that as an excuse for you to go ashore.

> It's not very nice when the chief engineer comes up on the bridge and says "You four women, on the bridge now. Which one [of you is responsible for this]? Look what I found, just blown out at me through the pipe – it's a sanitary [item]".

> There are certain things you can do on board ship and certain things you can't. Best thing – put the bag over the side [... but ...] if you're caught doing that, the company could been fined thousands for people chucking rubbish over the side.

> Well, if you think of it, when a new woman joins the ship, she puts something down the toilet – engineers hate women for that week. They hate women because they've had to stick [...] shit everywhere, it's stinking. Happened to a ship I was on and the cadets had to clear it up. It doesn't help a woman at sea when someone does that. The engineers, they don't like you for a week and then it's back to normal.

Much larger numbers of women work on cruise and passenger vessels, with additional women aboard as passengers and tourists. The presence of such relatively large numbers of women, combined with comparatively frequent port calls and opportunities to go ashore, has perhaps made the issue of access to, and disposal of, sanitary products less of a problem. Nevertheless, tampons and sanitary towels are rarely available in crew shops on cruise ships, and, while they can be purchased in passenger shops, access to such stores is often restricted to specific hours or to higher-ranking crew. It was also observed during the collection of data that missions to seafarers do not always take women's needs into account by making feminine hygiene products available in their shops.

Thus, in both sectors of the industry, women seafarers are largely dependent on the opportunity to go ashore and on having enough time to travel to local supermarkets to purchase these items.

In the cruise sector, women are rarely told how to dispose of sanitary products correctly. Although passenger toilets often have signs describing the correct methods of disposal and are equipped with sanitary bins, many crew toilets have no such advice or simply display warnings not to flush such items down the toilet. Most women reported that they disposed of sanitary products either in their own cabin bins or in sanitary bins in passengers' public toilets. Only women in senior ranks reported being supplied with sanitary disposal bags in their private accommodation.

Contraception, conception and general medical health

In the cargo sector, women rarely acknowledged engaging in any kind of sexual relationship or activity on board and so free access to contraception is not an issue of concern to them. In the cruise sector, however, sexual relationships were more regularly reported and most women said that condoms were available on board. These were often said to be located in public areas such as the crew bar, the ship's hospital or the crew laundry. The contraceptive pill was frequently reported to be available through the ship's doctor. One seafarer also reported sailing on a ship where the emergency contraceptive or "morning after" pill was available to crew members via the ship's doctor, and was very positive about this provision. However, access to the doctor for those in lower ranks is restricted and often not confidential: in some cases women have to fill in a form detailing the reason for their request to see the doctor, which then has to be signed by their supervisor. Such a lack of confidentiality can make going to see the doctor problematic for some women.

The public location of condoms aboard and the restrictions and lack of confidentiality regarding visits to ships' doctors may result in contraceptives and condoms being used less frequently. The reported level of sexual relationships among crew members while aboard suggests that company policies should address these issues if they are to prevent the spread of disease and unwanted pregnancies:

> [...] If the company finds out that you're pregnant and you haven't said anything about it, you'll be in trouble. [...] It's quite difficult going home earlier than planned and you won't have a job, especially if you're pregnant. It's quite hard to get a job back home, so you just hide it. I've heard that some women do commit abortion when it's an unwanted pregnancy. [...] I don't know how they do it. I haven't really asked about it. But I've heard stories about it, especially if they're married and they get pregnant on the ship. There's going to be trouble going home, with the husband asking, "How did you get pregnant?".

In both the cruise and cargo sectors, many women reported being required to take a pregnancy test prior to joining. Such tests are usually performed as part of the standard seafarers' medical examination. Women's understanding of company policy on conception varies and is sometimes confused. In the cruise sector, many women asserted that if a woman found out that she was pregnant aboard, she should immediately inform her supervisor, believing that this would lead to her being immediately dismissed. However, others feel that their company might allow a woman to sail for up to four months into the pregnancy. They consider that the likelihood of dismissal will vary, depending on the nature of the woman's work, specifically whether it is physically demanding. In the commercial sector, many companies have an "informal" policy relating to pregnancy and do not allow women to sail while pregnant. However, this policy is often not communicated to women aboard ship, who are left to formulate their own ideas about what happens should they become pregnant.

In the hotel sector, women are typically employed on single contracts, of which the length of service can vary between one and ten months. Most women seem to be unaware of any company policy on maternity leave. It is often believed that companies will accept women back on board after child-birth, as and when a place becomes available. However, none of the women interviewed was aware of any financial provisions made by the company for maternity leave. The prevalent belief is that a pregnancy results in a period of unpaid leave, with no guarantee of re-employment after the birth should the mother wish to go back to sea. In the marine sector, maternity benefits depend on both company policy and the flag of the ship. For example, German women sailing on German flagged ships appear to be entitled to full maternity benefits in line with German social security policy.

While at sea, those on board are largely dependent on fellow crew members for medical consultations and treatment. Cruise ships typically carry qualified medical personnel. However, as noted earlier, crew members often have limited access to a ship's medical staff and access is typically limited to very restricted hours, requiring authorization from a supervisor. Such regulations do not encourage good health nor the effective treatment of crew members. The working hours doctors set aside for treating crew members also often conflict with the working hours of seafarers.

This system of access has implications for confidentiality and sometimes results in crew members avoiding consultations for problems they feel are sensitive, punishable, or in some way stigmatizing.

Medical care aboard cargo vessels is generally provided by deck officers, who are responsible for providing advice and medical treatment to seafarers on board. Although this generally works well, there are occasions when such arrangements result in awkward situations for women, from the standpoint of either giving or receiving medical care. The following example is illustrative:

> I had one AB and he came to the dispensary room because something was wrong. He mentioned something being wrong with his stomach, maybe not the stomach. And I was second mate, and he was sitting there. "OK, what's wrong with your stomach?" "Well, you know, it's not quite the stomach." "Well, what is it then?" "Well", and the guy blushed all over, "it's the testicle, it's swollen". "Did you see prostitutes in the last port?" "No." So I said to myself, "What does he want me to do about it? Take a look or ask the chief officer?" But the chief officer was a stupid old guy and the crew didn't like him, "Not the chief officer, not the chief officer!" […] And I said, "I can take a look, if it's necessary." "It's swollen. Yes, it's painful." In the end, I gave him some mild painkillers and talked to the captain about it, who agreed that he had to see a doctor.

Summary

This chapter explored the experiences of women working aboard both cargo and cruise vessels in a variety of jobs. According to their accounts, women from developed countries, who often work in the marine department, often enter the industry because there is a seafarer in their family or they have a desire to "see the world". However, women in developing countries, who are well represented in the hotel sector, tend to be motivated by economic gain.

Women find that gaining access to maritime education is relatively problem-free and in certain countries some reported that they were encouraged to enrol. However, some MET staff still seem to be averse to having women in the industry and such attitudes are also reflected in the difficulties women experience in finding cadet or apprentice placements on vessels.

Once aboard vessels, as trainees or later as officers, women in the marine department reported difficulty in being initially accepted by their male colleagues and often find that they have to work particularly hard to "prove themselves" as willing and capable, occasionally in quite hostile circumstances. However, over time and as a result of their efforts, women are generally able to integrate themselves into crews and become accepted and appreciated by their colleagues. In the marine sector, many women feel that their promotion prospects are similar to those of men, although some companies are reluctant to promote women to more senior ranks, or indeed to employ women at all. In the hotel sector, differential access to promotion on the basis of gender is less apparent, and some women feel that promotion prospects are more closely associated with ethnicity than with gender.

Sexual harassment is a reality for many women in both the marine and hotel sectors. Their experiences range from persistent verbal harassment and inappropriate comments to physical assault. High-profile company sexual harassment policies in some parts of the cruise sector were found to be effective in both reducing incidents of sexual harassment and encouraging women to seek company support in such situations. In the commercial sector, few women reported the existence of company policies on sexual harassment and when they did complain about sexual harassment they did not always receive a satisfactory response.

Companies do not appear to address issues relating to menstruation effectively and for many women, particularly in the cargo sector, the purchase and disposal of sanitary items can be a source of considerable anxiety and distress.

Although sexual relationships aboard cargo ships were reported only infrequently, such relationships are a common feature of working life aboard cruise ships. Most cruise ships were reported to carry condoms and many women reported access to the contraceptive pill via ships' doctors. However, it was suggested that unwanted pregnancies do occur aboard cruise vessels and that some women risk their own health trying to get an abortion while continuing to work. Maternity leave in both sectors was reported to be scant, if not non-existent: many women in the cruise sector believe that pregnancy will result in immediate dismissal.

CONCLUSIONS AND RECOMMENDATIONS   6
.

Women in the workforce

Having collated and examined a variety of data, it is clear that women continue to constitute a very small part of the labour force of seafarers and that their distribution is highly skewed, with far higher proportions of women coming from parts of Europe than from the rest of the world. Given that there is a general decline in the overall numbers of European seafarers, this trend implies that the total proportion of women working in the industry's commercial sector can be expected to decline, rather than increase, in future years, all other things being equal. In the cruise sector, all the indications are that female participation rates will rise, especially among hotel staff.

Women are not only clustered in terms of their country of origin; within the seafarers' labour market, their distribution is highly segmented. Significantly higher numbers of women work in the passenger sector of the shipping industry and most of these women are employed in the hotel and catering side. Few women work in the marine department of the cruise sector and they are seriously under-represented in the marine department of the commercial sector.

Given the predicted shortage of navigation officers and engineers in the shipping industry as a whole and the high turnover of hotel staff in the cruise sector, women would appear to be an underexploited labour source. This is perhaps surprising as the companies employing women consistently referred to the quality and commitment of female staff and the general benefits of having a more gender-balanced shipboard workforce. However, the research revealed that a number of strong stereotypes pertaining to the abilities and characteristics of women continue to pervade the industry at all levels and in all sectors. Such prejudices are overlaid with further stereotypes relating to ethnicity. Thus, for some companies, employing "Western" women is less problematic than employing women from other regions. Additionally, and despite women's positive track record in this area, some companies have reservations about the ability of women to supervise mixed nationality crews.

There are insufficient numbers of women seafarers to allow for accurate statistical comparisons of male and female retention rates within the industry. However, despite the perception in some quarters of the industry that women seafarers stay at sea for shorter periods than their male colleagues, our evidence suggests that the retention rates of women coming from OECD countries, where most women in the marine sector are employed, are broadly comparable.

Policies and practices relating to the employment of women

The data collected for the study indicate that most companies have no specific policies relating to the employment of women. A number of these companies unofficially reject applications from women seafarers. There is also evidence to suggest that in some companies women are barred from specific, and mostly supervisory, posts, such as those of bosun and chief engineer. Many companies use crewing agents to recruit their staff and, whereas "parent" company policy might not discriminate against women, there is evidence to suggest that in some parts of the world crewing agents do not recruit, or remunerate, seafarers on an equal basis.

Despite the general underutilization of female labour, there are companies that have taken advantage of the many benefits that can accrue from employing women seafarers and have recruited a number of them in all ranks. However, even those companies with women seafarers on their books have not generally formulated a set of policies concerning their employment. Nevertheless, they tend to apply existing policies evenly, regardless of gender, such as policies relating to family members or partners sailing with seafarers. Some companies across the industry have taken active steps to support seafaring couples by synchronizing contracts of employment and vessels, where requested.

Just as many companies employing women on an equal opportunities basis have no specific policies with regard to their recruitment and employment, so too have many overlooked the need for the development and implementation of gender-related policies and practices on board their vessels. The research has highlighted a need for policies addressing issues relating to sexual harassment, menstruation, pregnancy, contraception, maternity, and sexual and general medical health. In the cruise sector, where the majority of women are employed, there are some companies that have developed policies and practices relating to some of these issues, with positive effect.

In our sample, we found that a number of cruise companies have instituted high-profile policies on sexual harassment and give specific employee training on this issue. In these cases, the seafarers interviewed reported fewer incidents of sexual harassment and increased levels of confidence in dealing with cases that do arise. Within all sectors of the industry, policies and practices relating to pregnancy and maternity benefits vary considerably between companies. Company responses to staff becoming pregnant range from immediate dismissal to offers of alternative shore-side employment. In some instances, policies on pregnancy and maternity benefits are governed by regulations imposed by the conditions of registration (flag State) of the ship. These tend to benefit women seafarers and it was noted that, as increasing numbers of companies "flag out" their fleets, so the conditions of employment for many women seafarers will deteriorate. This situation is exacerbated by the increased tendency for seafarers to be employed on short-term contracts, which, in the main, enables employers to avoid issues relating to maternity benefits altogether.

Our evidence suggests that, in some parts of the world, more women are enrolling in MET institutions, which may go some way to help address the predicted deficit in the future supply of officers in the marine sector. And the indications are that a rise in women's participation is likely to go beyond merely "filling a gap" in terms of its benefits. Although women continue to experience some difficulty in accessing company training placements aboard vessels, those who do succeed and complete their training have very positive attitudes to their work. Such attitudes manifest themselves in the overall performance of women seafarers, who are widely reported, by the shipowners and managers employing them, to perform well above the average for seafarers at all levels in the industry. Support for the recruitment and retention of women seafarers would, therefore, appear to be not only beneficial but also highly advantageous to the shipping community.

Recommendations

In making recommendations we are conscious that the shipping industry is far from homogeneous. The maritime community is made up of a number of constituent parts, including: non-governmental organizations (NGOs) such as the ILO and the IMO; welfare bodies, such as the Apostleship of the Sea and the International Seafarers' Assistance Network; trade unions; trade and employer associations; MET institutions; and individual shipowners and managers. These recommendations may not all be relevant to these individual groups and we have, therefore, attempted to indicate which recommendations we believe would be best dealt with by the different sectors of the industry. It is not our intention to be overly prescriptive, however, and in making these recommendations we recognize that shipping companies range in size and character and operate in different sectors of the freight market. Such variables inevitably have an impact on the scope for implementing change, particularly if significant additional costs are entailed. Notwithstanding such constraints, there is still much that can be done across the industry, particularly by individual companies, in relation to the employment of women seafarers. Many of the steps that can be taken to improve the situation of women working at sea entail little cost, and such outlay as may be required can easily be justified in terms of future benefits.

The ILO/trade unions

Given the positive experiences of many employers who have been proactive in recruiting and supporting women seafarers, efforts should be made to disseminate these experiences, with a view to reducing the prevalence of gender stereotypes within the industry.

Companies

In order to minimize the difficulties encountered by lone female cadets, as reported in Chapter 5, we would advise companies recruiting women to make every effort to place female cadets on ships with senior female officers, preferably captains, or, when this is impossible, with other female trainees or serving seafarers.

The confusion identified in some of the research findings with regard to company policies and practices could be reduced by extending or introducing induction training for all seafarers covering company policy relating to non-discrimination, equal opportunities, sexual harassment and the disposal of sanitary items. This could have the additional benefit of reducing the incidence of harassment and discrimination on board as it would highlight company commitment to equal opportunities and might thus deter potential "offenders".

Companies and trade unions

As a matter of priority, companies should make provisions for the purchase and discreet disposal of sanitary items aboard all cruise and cargo vessels, since this single issue causes stress and anxiety to women seafarers, particularly to younger, less-experienced women. Trade unions are likely to be required to take a proactive role in educating companies on the importance of this practical issue, since many individual managers in the industry are reluctant to broach this taboo topic.

Trade unions could also help promote the case for improved confidential access to medical staff for women employed in the cruise sector, and for making the contraceptive pill readily available on board. Although there is no reason why cargo vessels should not also carry the Pill, as a minimum requirement we would recommend that they, as well as their cruise-sector counterparts, stock a supply of the emergency contraceptive or "morning after" pill, which should be made readily and confidentially available to all women seafarers, subject to standard medical guidance.

Companies/trade unions/the ILO

As there is so much variation in maternity benefits and rights available to shore-based and land-based employees, even within the same company, further consideration should be given to developing an improved and consistent approach across the shipping industry, which would be more closely comparable to conditions offered to shore workers.

Companies/trade unions/the ILO/training institutions

Sexual harassment policies should be developed across the industry in line with the best practice of some existing companies. These policies should be accompanied by dedicated training courses. It would be beneficial if awareness of sexual harassment, a subject on which there is often much confusion and misunderstanding, could be raised via special training for all serving seafarers and shore-based personnel across the industry. As a minimum, however, sexual harassment should be an integral part of the curricula of all establishments offering cadet training and education so that both male and female cadets have the opportunity to consider the subject while at college.

Training institutions/trade unions/the ILO/trade and employer associations

Although some MET institutions have been successful in recruiting small numbers of women to their courses, they are often hampered by the reluctance of employers to take on women trainees. Our evidence suggests that companies need to be targeted by educational and advertising means to encourage them to offer greater numbers of cadet placements to women. The ILO, trade unions and employer and trade associations could take a leading role in promoting women's employment at sea, while training institutions should continue to approach employers and actively seek placement opportunities for their female cadets.

Registries

Regulatory best practice with regard to recruitment, training, maternity benefit and the protection and promotion of women should be mirrored across all registries.

Recommendations for further research

As highlighted in Chapter 1, very little research on women seafarers has been carried out. This study has attempted to explore and document systematically related policies, practice, employment conditions and the experiences of women working at sea. During the process of conducting this research, our attention was drawn to a number of areas that would benefit from further, dedicated research. In particular, we would recommend that:

- a longitudinal cohort study of male and female cadets be carried out in order to explore the particular issues confronting new entrants to the industry and to address the problem of high levels of attrition during cadetships.

- a method be considered to establish comparative male and female levels of recruitment and retention, and that a central database be developed to monitor participation rates of men and women on an annual basis and across all sectors of the industry. Such a database should provide comparative data to allow for effective analysis so that robust information is available for the formulation of policy decisions regarding recruitment and retention.

QUESTIONNAIRE FOR
GOVERNMENT AGENCIES

The name of your organization: . . . .

I   Data

1   Please complete the following table with the total number of seafarers included in the national registry, taking into account gender and category.

		Number of seafarers	
		Male	Female
Officers	Deck	. . . .	. . . .
	Engine	. . . .	. . . .
	Hotel	. . . .	. . . .
	Other	. . . .	. . . .
Ratings	Deck	. . . .	. . . .
	Engine	. . . .	. . . .
	Hotel/Catering	. . . .	. . . .
	Other	. . . .	. . . .

II Policy

2   Does your organization have a specific policy relating to the employment of women?

    (1) Yes ❑   (2) No ❑

    Could you explain briefly the reasons? . . . .

    . . . .

If your organization does not have any policy in this respect, we would like to thank you for the time taken.

3   Is your policy designed to encourage or discourage the employment of women seafarers?

    (1) Yes ❑   (2) No ❑

    Could you explain briefly why? . . . .

    . . . .

4   On which areas is your policy more focused?

    (1) Recruitment   ❑

    (2) Training   ❑

    (3) Retention   ❑

    (4) Pregnancy leave   ❑

    (5) Maternity leave   ❑

    (6) On-board working conditions/health and safety   ❑

    (7) Other, could you specify . . . .

    . . . .

5   Would it be possible for your organization to send to SIRC a copy of the policy?

    (1) Yes ❑   (2) No ❑   (3) A copy is enclosed with the questionnaire ❑

Thank you very much for your interest and cooperation.

QUESTIONNAIRE FOR TRADE UNIONS

I	Data

1 Please complete the following table with the total number of seafarers who are members of your union, taking into account gender and category.

		Number of seafarers	
		Male	Female
Officers	Deck	. . . .	. . . .
	Engine	. . . .	. . . .
	Hotel	. . . .	. . . .
	Other, specify	. . . .	. . . .
		. . . .	. . . .
Ratings	Deck	. . . .	. . . .
	Engine	. . . .	. . . .
	Hotel/Catering	. . . .	. . . .
	Other, specify	. . . .	. . . .
		. . . .	. . . .

II Policy

2 Does your organization have a specific policy relating to the employment of women?

(1) Yes ❑   (2) No ❑

If "No", we would like to thank you for the time taken. Otherwise, please proceed to the following question.

3 Is your policy designed to encourage or discourage the employment of women seafarers?

(1) Yes ❑   (2) No ❑

Could you specify the reasons? . . . .

. . . .

. . . .

4 On which areas is your policy more focused?

(1) Recruitment   ❑

(2) Training   ❑

(3) Retention   ❑

(4) Maternity leave   ❑

(5) On-board working conditions/health and safety   ❑

(6) Sexual harassment   ❑

(7) Other, could you specify . . . .

. . . .

5 Would it be possible for your organization to send to SIRC a copy of the policy?

(1) Yes ❑   (2) No ❑   (3) A copy is enclosed with the questionnaire ❑

Thank you very much for your interest and cooperation.

QUESTIONNAIRE FOR EMPLOYERS APPENDIX III

I   Company information

Is your company mainly a:

(a) Shipowner?   ❑

(b) Ship operator?   ❑

(c) Ship manager?   ❑

(d) Crew manager?   ❑

1   What is the total number of vessels
owned/managed/crewed by your company?   . . . .

2   What are the flags used by the vessels?

National flag   . . . .

Other first registers   . . . .

Second registers   . . . .

Open registers   . . . .

3   What are the trading regions in which your vessels operate?   . . . .

. . . .

. . . .

---

4   What is the average size of your fleet?

- Less than 3,000 GT   ❑

- Between 3,000 and 5,000 GT   ❑

- Between 5,000 and 10,000 GT   ❑

- Between 10,000 and 20,000 GT   ❑

- Between 20,000 and 30,000 GT   ❑

- Between 30,000 and 50,000 GT   ❑

- More than 50,000 GT   ❑

5   Could you please complete the table below with the total number of seafarers employed by your company, taking into account the type of vessel, gender and rank.

(a) Cargo vessels

		Number of seafarers	
		Male	Female
Officers	Deck	. . . .	. . . .
	Engine	. . . .	. . . .
	Other, specify	. . . .	. . . .
		. . . .	. . . .
Ratings	Deck	. . . .	. . . .
	Engine	. . . .	. . . .
	Catering	. . . .	. . . .
	Other, specify	. . . .	. . . .
		. . . .	. . . .

(b) Ferries

		Number of seafarers	
		Male	Female
Officers	Deck	. . . .	. . . .
	Engine	. . . .	. . . .
	Hotel, Catering	. . . .	. . . .
	Other, specify	. . . .	. . . .
		. . . .	. . . .
Ratings	Deck	. . . .	. . . .
	Engine	. . . .	. . . .
	Hotel, Catering	. . . .	. . . .
	Other, specify	. . . .	. . . .
		. . . .	. . . .

(c) Passenger/Cruise vessels

		Number of seafarers	
		Male	Female
Officers	Deck	. . . .	. . . .
	Engine	. . . .	. . . .
	Hotel, Catering	. . . .	. . . .
	Other, specify	. . . .	. . . .
		. . . .	. . . .
Ratings	Deck	. . . .	. . . .
	Engine	. . . .	. . . .
	Hotel, Catering	. . . .	. . . .
	Other, specify	. . . .	. . . .
		. . . .	. . . .

6. Are male and female seafarers of the same rank and nationality paid the same rates?

(1) Yes ❑   (2) No ❑

II   Policy

7   Does your company have a specific policy relating to the employment of women?

(1) Yes ❏   (2) No ❏

If the answer to this question was "No", please proceed to question 11.

8   Is your policy designed to encourage or discourage the employment of women?

(1) Yes ❏   (2) No ❏

9   On which areas is your policy more focused?

(1) Recruitment   ❏

(2) Training   ❏

(3) Retention   ❏

(4) Pregnancy leave   ❏

(5) Maternity leave   ❏

(6) On-board working conditions/health and safety   ❏

(7) Sexual harassment   ❏

(8) Other, please specify . . . .

. . . .

10   Would it be possible for your organization to send to SIRC a copy of the policy?

(1) Yes ❏   (2) No ❏   (3) A copy is enclosed with the questionnaire ❏

11   What is the highest rank that a woman seafarer can be appointed in your company while working at sea? . . . .

12   What is the highest ranking post that a woman has ever been appointed to in your company? . . . .

13   Are there any positions in which you would NOT employ a woman?

    (1) Yes ❑   (2) No ❑

If the answer to this question was "No", please proceed to question 16.

14   Which posts wouldn't you employ women in?

    (1) Master   ❑

    (2) Chief engineer   ❑

    (3) Chief mate   ❑

    (4) Bosun   ❑

    (5) Other, please specify . . . .

    . . . .

15   Why wouldn't you employ women in these posts?

    . . . .

    . . . .

    . . . .

16   Does your company have future plans to encourage the recruitment and retention of women seafarers?

    (1) Yes ❑   (2) No ❑

17   If your answer to the previous question was "Yes", would you please specify.

    . . . .

    . . . .

18   Do you have any further information or views that you think would be useful for the ILO regarding the employment of women at sea?

    . . . .

    . . . .

Thank you very much for your interest and cooperation.

QUESTIONNAIRE FOR MET INSTITUTIONS

I   Data

1   Could you please complete the following table, giving the total number of students attending courses at your institution.

		Number of students	
		Male	Female
Officers	Deck		
	1st year	. . . .	. . . .
	2nd year	. . . .	. . . .
	3rd year	. . . .	. . . .
	4th year (if applicable)	. . . .	. . . .
	Upgrading	. . . .	. . . .
	Engine		
	1st year	. . . .	. . . .
	2nd year	. . . .	. . . .
	3rd year	. . . .	. . . .
	4th year (if applicable)	. . . .	. . . .
	Upgrading	. . . .	. . . .
	Hotel		
	1st year	. . . .	. . . .
	2nd year	. . . .	. . . .
	Upgrading	. . . .	. . . .

		Number of students	
		Male	Female
Ratings	Deck		
	Initial	. . . .	. . . .
	Upgrading	. . . .	. . . .
	Engine		
	Initial	. . . .	. . . .
	Upgrading	. . . .	. . . .
	Hotel/Catering		
	Initial	. . . .	. . . .
	Upgrading	. . . .	. . . .
Other, specify			
. . . .		. . . .	. . . .
. . . .		. . . .	. . . .

II Policy

2 Does your organization have a specific policy relating to the recruitment of women?

(1) Yes ❑   (2) No ❑

If the answer to this question was "No", could you specify why such a policy does not exist? . . . .

. . . .

. . . .

. . . .

If your organization does not have any specific policy, we would like to thank you for the time taken and your interest in this study.

3   Is your policy designed to encourage or discourage the recruitment of women

as future seafarers? . . . .

. . . .

Could you specify the reasons? . . . .

. . . .

4   On which areas is your policy more focused?

(1) Recruitment   ❑

(2) Training   ❑

(3) Retention   ❑

(4) On-board working conditions/health and safety   ❑

(5) Sexual harassment   ❑

(6) Other, could you specify . . . .

. . . .

. . . .

5   Would it be possible for your organization to send to SIRC a copy of the policy?

(1) Yes ❑   (2) No ❑   (3) A copy is enclosed with the questionnaire ❑

Thank you very much for your interest and cooperation.

QUESTIONNAIRE FOR WOMEN SEAFARERS

Background

1   How old are you?

Under 16   ❑

16–25 years   ❑

26–35 years   ❑

36–45 years   ❑

46 years or older   ❑

2   What is your nationality?

American   ❑

British   ❑

Other Western European . . . . *(please write in)*

Ukrainian   ❑

Other Eastern European . . . . *(please write in)*

Filipino   ❑

Indonesian   ❑

Indian   ❑

Chinese   ❑

Other Asian . . . . *(please write in)*

Other . . . . *(please write in)*

3   What is your current marital status?

Married ❑

Never married ❑

Separated ❑

Widowed ❑

Divorced ❑

Co-habiting ❑

4   How many times have you been married?

Never ❑

Once ❑

Twice ❑

More than twice ❑

5   What is your husband/partner's occupation? (*please write in*)

. . . .

My husband/partner is not in paid employment ❑

I do not have a husband/partner ❑

6   How many children do you have?

None ❑

One ❑

Two ❑

More than two ❑

7   How old are they?

The oldest . . . . years

The youngest . . . . years

8   Do you have any other extended family living in your home (for example, your parents or grandparents)? (*please write in*)

. . . .

. . . .

9   What is the MAIN reason you work at sea? (*please tick one box only*)

To see other countries   ❏

To earn more money   ❏

To satisfy desire for adventure   ❏

Could not find other job ashore   ❏

Other (*please write in*) . . . .

. . . .

10   What is your position on this ship?

Deck officer . . . . (*please write in* rank)

Engineer . . . . (*please write in* rank)

Cabin stewardess   ❏

Restaurant waitress   ❏

Bar waitress   ❏

Other rating . . . . (*please write in* rank)

Other . . . . (*please write in*)

11   How long have you been working at sea? (*please write in*)

. . . . years . . . . months

Experience at sea

12 As a woman on board ship, do you feel that the standards of work expected of you are:

- the same as those expected of your male colleagues
  (who are doing the same job as you)?   ❑

- higher than those expected of your male colleagues
  (who are doing the same job as you)?   ❑

- lower than those expected of your male colleagues
  (who are doing the same job as you)?   ❑

13 Have you had any of the following problems with your colleagues?
    (*please tick all that apply*)

	Male	Female
Bullying	❑	❑
Verbal harassment (non-sexual)	❑	❑
Physical harassment (non-sexual)	❑	❑
Verbal harassment (sexual)	❑	❑
Physical harassment (sexual)	❑	❑
Other, please specify	❑	❑

If your answer is negative, please proceed to question 18.

14 Which ranks have caused you problems? (*please tick all that apply*)

	Male	Female
Master	❑	❑
Officer	❑	❑
Rating (Deck/Engine)	❑	❑
Staff in hotel/catering	❑	❑
Passenger	❑	❑
Other	❑	❑

15 Have the people who have caused you problems been:

	Male	Female
The same nationality as you?	❑	❑
A different nationality to you?	❑	❑
Both?	❑	❑

16 When you have a problem/problems, how do you usually cope?

Keep it to yourself	❑
Share it with your family	❑
Get support from colleagues	❑
Report it to your immediate manager	❑
Report it to your captain	❑
Report it to your crewing (manning) agent	❑

Other . . . . (please write in)

17 If you reported a problem/s with a colleague's behaviour, were you happy with the way it was handled?

Always happy	❑
Sometimes happy	❑
Never happy	❑

18 Would you encourage another woman to do the same job as you?

Yes ❑ No ❑

Company support

19 Does your company have an equal opportunities policy?

   Yes ❑   No ❑   Don't know ❑

20 Does your company have a sexual harassment policy?

   Yes ❑   No ❑   Don't know ❑

21 Does your company provide training to deal with sexual harassment?

   Yes ❑   No ❑   Don't know ❑

22 Does your company provide paid maternity leave?

   Yes ❑   No ❑   Don't know ❑

23 Does your company allow your husband/partner to sail with you?

   Yes ❑   No ❑   Don't know ❑

   Not applicable/I do not have a husband/partner.   ❑

24 Does your company allow the wives/partners of your male colleagues of the same rank of you to sail?

   Yes ❑   No ❑   Don't know ❑

25 Does your company allow you to continue working in this job if you are pregnant?

   Yes ❑   No ❑   Don't know ❑

26 If "Yes", how far into your pregnancy are you allowed to work? . . . . months

27 Does your company insist on a negative pregnancy test before you join the ship?

   Yes ❑   No ❑   Don't know ❑

28 Are you paid the same wages as men of the same nationality as you doing the same job as you?

   Yes ❑   No ❑   Don't know ❑

   Not applicable/
   There are not any men of the same nationality doing the same job as me. ❑

29 Do you feel your chances of promotion (while working at sea) are:

The same as your male colleagues? ❏

Higher than your male colleagues? ❏

Less than your male colleagues? ❏

30 Why do you think this is? (*please write in*)...............................

. . . .

. . . .

31 Do you feel that your uniform is practical for the job you do?

Yes ❏   No ❏   Not applicable/I do not have to wear a uniform ❏

32 Does your company make special requirements on your appearance (for example, weight restrictions, hair, etc.)?

Yes ❏   No ❏

33 If "Yes", what are these? (*please write in*) . . . .

. . . .

. . . .

33 Does your ship's bond/store sell:

	Yes	No	Don't know
Tampons?	❏	❏	❏
Sanitary towels?	❏	❏	❏
Other toiletries for women? (e.g. deodorants, moisturizers, etc.)	❏	❏	❏

34 Is there adequate provision for female crew for the disposal of tampons/sanitary towels on board?

Yes ❏   No ❏

35 Do you have access to female-only toilets?

Yes ❏   No ❏

36 Do you have access to female-only showers?

Yes ☐   No ☐

37 What kind of accommodation do you have on board?

A single cabin to yourself   ☐

You share a cabin with one other person   ☐

You share a cabin with more than one person   ☐

You share a bed/bunk with another person   ☐

Other . . . . (please write in)

38 Does your cabin have a lock that you are able to use?

Yes ☐   No ☐

Union support

39 Are you a union member?

Yes ☐   No ☐

41 If "Yes", what is your union? (please write in)

. . . .

. . . .

42 Do you feel your union pays adequate attention to the specific issues facing women seafarers?

Yes ☐   No ☐   Don't know ☐

43 If not, which issues do you think they should give more attention to?

(please write in) . . . .

. . . .

. . . .

. . . .

Social life aboard ship

44 During your free time aboard are you most likely to be:

Alone? ❏

Socializing with female colleagues? ❏

Socializing with male colleagues? ❏

Socializing with both male and female colleagues? ❏

45 Do male/female seafarers have segregated accommodation areas?

Yes, separate decks ❏

Yes, separate areas of the same deck ❏

No ❏

46 Are male seafarers allowed access to female accommodation areas?

Yes, all the time ❏   Yes, sometimes ❏   No ❏

47 Are female seafarers allowed access to male accommodation areas?

Yes, all the time ❏   Yes, sometimes ❏   No ❏

48 How long do you think you will carry on working at sea?

Until saved enough money ❏

Until marriage ❏

Until have children ❏

Until retirement ❏

Other . . . . (please write in)

Thank you for your help.

INTERVIEW SCHEDULE: GOVERNMENT AGENCIES

Background about the organization
 Responsibilities
  Issuance of certificates
  Renewal of certificates
  Examination of seafarers
  Medical examination
   Any particular aspect regarding limitation of employment due to pregnancy
 Number of seafarers registered (male/female)
  Distribution by ranks
  Relationship with MET institutions

Employment
 Official policies to attract young people to a seafaring profession
 Official policies regarding the employment of women at sea
 Unofficial policies on employment of women at sea
 National policies regarding:
  Maternity leave
  Pregnancy leave
 Are the above-mentioned policies applicable to women seafarers?
  If so, in which way?
 Data on retention rates of women seafarers
 Information regarding the employment of former women seafarers
  Where are they employed now?
  Policies to facilitate the integration of former women seafarers into shore-based activities
 Identified constraints in the employment of women at sea
 Identified benefits in the employment of women at sea

Strategies adopted in the past to increase the employment of women at sea
Policies in place to make life at sea more friendly for women
Posts at sea restricted to women

Suggestions

How to promote/integrate women's employment at sea

Background about the organization
  Role of the organization
  Number of women members
Percentage of women members compared with male members
    Number and percentage of women in the secretariat of the trade union
    Does the trade union have any special commission to deal with women's affairs?

Seafaring profession
    Official policies to attract young people to a seafaring profession
    Official policies to attract women to a seafaring profession
    Unofficial policies to attract women to a seafaring profession
    Data on retention rates of women seafarers
    Identified constraints in the employment of women at sea
    Identified benefits in the employment of women at sea
    Strategies adopted in the past to increase the employment of women at sea
    Complaints made by women
        What type of complaints?
        How does the trade union deal with complaints from women?
    Policies of the trade union regarding:
        Maternity leave
        Pregnancy leave
    Information regarding women who have left the seafaring profession
        Where are they working now?
        Reasons for leaving the seafaring profession

Suggestions
    How to promote/integrate women's employment at sea

Background about the organization

    Number of ships owned/managed/crewed

    Ship types

    Ship flags

    Trading region

    Average size of crews

    Total numbers of seafarers employed

    Nationalities employed

- officers
- ratings

Employment of women

    Policy regarding employment of women

    Number of women currently employed – ranks, length of service, age, departments, marital status, nationality, etc.

    Number of women employed in the past – when, how many, career histories, what happened to them?

    Retention rates of women seafarers past/present. Comparison with male retention rates?

    Experiences of employing women

Female-friendly policies and practices

    Policies to protect women aboard ship

    Policies with regard to pregnancy

    Policies with regard to maternity leave

    Provision for women aboard ship – policy/practices relating to items kept in the bonded store

    Provision for disposal of sanitary items, etc.?

    Can husbands/partners sail on ships? Are rules the same as for wives?

Can children sail on ships? Are rules the same for male/female seafarers?

Other policies/practices introduced by the company

Attitude to future employment of women

Plans to employ women in the future – why/why not?

Abilities of women seafarers – positive/negative

Cost-effectiveness of women seafarers?

Constraints on employing women – e.g. attitudes of owners, restrictions imposed by other bodies (e.g. trade unions/governments, etc.)

Benefits/disadvantages of employing women

Special strategies past/present to encourage or support the employment of women?

Have any been adopted? – explore reasons for answer

Have any been considered? – explore reasons

Other issues

Other relevant issues employers may wish to raise

INTERVIEW SCHEDULE: MET INSTITUTIONS

Background about the organization
    Courses available
    Academic degrees awarded
    Number of women attending the different courses
        Initial courses
        Upgrading courses
    Medical examination before entering
        Any particular tests for women candidates
    Retention rate of women during their studies
        Any differences regarding male students

Seafaring profession
    Official policies to attract young people to a seafaring profession
    Official policies to attract women to a seafaring profession
    Unofficial policies to attract women to a seafaring profession
    Data on retention rates of women seafarers
    Identified constraints in the employment of women at sea
    Identified benefits in the employment of women at sea
    Strategies adopted in the past to increase the numbers of women employed at sea
    Information regarding the performance of female students compared with male students

Suggestions
    How to promote/integrate women's employment at sea

Background
Age
Nationality
Qualifications – school and nautical
Current home/previous homes/birthplace
Occupations of parents
Occupations of siblings
Seafarer relatives/friends prior to becoming a seafarer?
Marital/family status
Occupation of husband/partner

Career history
Companies/ship types/flags of ships/nationalities worked with/for
Length of service with current and previous companies
Rank, previous ranks and length of service in each rank
Company training in different companies
Self-funded training

Getting into the maritime industry
Motivation – why?
Method of entry – how?
Ease/difficulty of entry
Attitude of family/friends to career choice
Initial expectations
Initial experiences

Experiences of training
Initial training
Further training

Support by trade union

Initial support

Ongoing and past support

Experiences of sailing

Size of crews sailed with

Types of voyage – deep sea/short sea trade, etc.

Types of accommodation – personal and general facilities

Gender composition of crews

Nationality of crews sailed with

Advantages and disadvantages of being a woman seafarer

Attitude of other seafarers?

Attitude of shore-based people – employers/friends/families/missions/port
workers, etc.?

Risks?

Other problems/benefits?

Working life on board ship

Working relationships with colleagues

Standards of work expected as a woman – same as male colleagues/higher/
lower?

Bad/good experiences

Social life on board ship

Issues facing women

Own social life and experiences on board

Social isolation/social solidarity?

Bad/good experiences?

Company support

Ship-based women-friendly policies – e.g. sexual harassment policy, policy
relating to husband/partner/children?

Ship-based women-friendly practices – e.g. female-friendly bonded store items
available, sanitary disposal facilities, private washing facilities, personal safety
(locks on doors – who else has keys?, etc.)

Requirement for women-friendly policies/practices at sea?

Problems experienced at sea and company response?

Company shore-based women-friendly policies, e.g. promotion prospects,
training provision, maternity leave, etc.?

Relationships ashore

Support from family

Support to family

Ability to communicate with family

Attitude of partner/children to career/length of absence, etc.

How can life at sea be improved for women?

Things that could/should be done by companies/trade unions/training
institutions/seafarers

Future plans

Short term

Medium term

Long term

WORLD BANK COUNTRY RATINGS APPENDIX XI

Low-income countries:

India	Ukraine

Lower middle-income economies:

Bulgaria	China	Jamaica	Latvia	Peru
Philippines	Romania	Russian Federation	Sri Lanka	Thailand

Upper middle-income economies:

Chile	Czech Republic	Isle of Man	Malaysia
Mexico	Poland	South Africa	

High-income and OECD members:

Australia	Austria	Belgium	Canada	Denmark
Finland	France	Germany	Greece	Hong Kong
Ireland	Italy	Japan	New Zealand	Norway
Portugal	Singapore	Slovenia	Spain	Sweden
United Kingdom	United States			

Equal opportunity and treatment in respect of employment and occupation

ILO instruments

- Declaration of Philadelphia Concerning the Aims and Purpose of the International Labour Organization – articles II(a) and III(j)
- Declaration of Fundamental Principles and Rights at Work and its Follow-Up – Preamble and paragraph 2(d)
- Discrimination (Employment and Occupation) Convention, 1958 (No. 111) – articles 1.1(a), 2 and 5.2
- Discrimination (Employment and Occupation) Recommendation, 1958 (No. 111) – paragraphs 1(1), 2(a) and (b) and 6
- Social Policy (Basic Aims and Standards) Convention, 1962 (No. 117) – article 14.1 and 14.2
- Employment Policy Convention, 1964 (No. 122) – article 1.1 and 1.2
- Employment Policy Recommendation, 1964 (No. 122) – paragraphs 1(1) and 1(2), 29(1) and (2)(g)
- Employment Policy (Supplementary Provisions) Recommendation, 1984 (No. 169) – paragraph 7
- Human Resources Development Recommendation, 1975 (No. 150) – paragraph 54(1) and (2)(b)
- Workers with Family Responsibilities Recommendation, 1981 (No. 165) – paragraphs 7 and 8(2)
- Termination of Employment Convention, 1982 (No. 158) – article 5(d)
- Vocational Rehabilitation and Employment (Disabled Persons) Convention, 1983 (No. 159) – article 4
- Vocational Rehabilitation and Employment (Disabled Persons) Recommendation, 1983 (No. 168) – paragraph 8

- Employment Promotion and Protection against Unemployment Convention, 1988 (No. 168) – articles 6 and 8.1
- Night Work Convention, 1990 (No. 171) – article 1(b)
- Night Work Recommendation, 1990 (No. 178) – paragraph 1(b)
- Maternity Protection Convention, 2000 (No. 183) – articles 8 and 9

Other international instruments

- Convention of the Elimination of All Forms of Discrimination against Women – article 11.1(b) and (c)
- International Covenant on Economic, Social and Cultural Rights – article 6.1
- Beijing Platform for Action – paragraph 178(c)

Pay sufficient for the maintenance of themselves and their children in accordance with a suitable standard of living

ILO instruments

- Protocol of 1990 to the Night Work (Women) Convention (Revised), 1948 (No. 89) – article 2.3(b)
- Protection of Wages Convention, 1949 (No. 95) – article 10.2
- Maternity Protection Convention (Revised), 1952 (No. 103) – article 4.2
- Maternity Protection Recommendation, 1952 (No. 95) – paragraph 2(3)
- Plantations Convention, 1958 (No. 110) – article 48(2)
- Social Policy (Basic Aims and Standards) Convention, 1962 (No. 117) – article 5
- Minimum Wage Fixing Convention, 1970 (No. 131) – article 3(a)
- Minimum Age Recommendation, 1973 (No. 146) – paragraph 13(1)(a)
- Employment Promotion and Protection against Unemployment Convention, 1988 (No. 168) – article 16
- Maternity Protection Convention, 2000 (No. 183) – articles 6 and 7

Other international instruments

- Universal Declaration of Human Rights – articles 23.3 and 25.1
- International Covenant on Economic, Social and Cultural Rights – articles 7(a)(i) and (ii) and 11.1

Equal pay for work of equal value

ILO instruments

- ILO Constitution – Preamble
- Equal Remuneration Convention, 1951 (No. 100) – articles 1, 2 and 3

- Equal Remuneration Recommendation, 1951 (No. 90) – paragraphs 1, 2, 3(1), 5 and 6
- Discrimination (Employment and Occupation) Recommendation, 1958 (No. 111) – paragraph 2(b)(v)
- Social Policy (Basic Aims and Standards) Convention, 1962 (No. 117) – article 14.1(I) and 14.2
- Minimum Age Recommendation, 1973 (No. 146) – paragraph 13(1)(a)
- Night Work Recommendation, 1990 (No. 178) – paragraph 8(1)(a)

Other international instruments

- Universal Declaration of Human Rights – article 23.2
- Convention on the Elimination of All Forms of Discrimination against Women – article 11.1(d)
- International Covenant on Economic, Social and Cultural Rights – article 7(a)(I)

Equality of access to vocational training

- Declaration of Philadelphia Concerning the Aims and Purpose of the International Labour Organization – article III(j)
- Discrimination (Employment and Occupation) Recommendation, 1958 (No. 111) – paragraph 2(b)(ii)
- Social Policy (Basic Aims and Standards) Convention, 1962 (No. 117) – article 14.1(d)
- Paid Educational Leave Convention, 1974 (No. 140) – articles 2 and 8
- Human Resources Development Convention, 1975 (No. 142) – article 1.1 and 1.5
- Rural Workers' Organizations Recommendation, 1975 (No. 149) – paragraphs 16(c) and 17(1)
- Human Resources Development Recommendation, 1975 (No. 150) – paragraphs 4(4), 5(2) and 54
- Workers with Family Responsibilities Recommendation, 1981 (No. 165) – paragraph 12
- Employment Policy (Supplementary Provisions) Recommendation, 1984 (No. 169) – paragraph 16
- Night Work Recommendation, 1990 (No. 178) – paragraphs 20 and 22

Other international instruments

- Convention on the Elimination of All Forms of Discrimination against Women – articles 10(a) and (e) and 11.1(c)

Equal rights to freedom of association and the right to collective bargaining in the workplace

ILO instruments

- Declaration on Fundamental Principles and Rights at Work and its Follow-Up – paragraph 2(a)
- Freedom of Association and Protection of the Right to Organize Convention, 1948 (No. 87)
- Plantations Convention, 1958 (No. 110) – articles 54, 62 and 70
- Social Policy (Basic Aims and Standards) Convention, 1962 (No. 117) – article 14.1(h)
- Rural Workers' Organizations Convention, 1975 (No. 141) – articles 3.1 and 3.2, and 4
- Rural Workers' Organizations Recommendation, 1975 (No. 149) – paragraphs 4, 8(1) and 2(a)
- Termination of Employment Convention, 1982 (No. 158) – article 5(a)

Other international instruments

- Universal Declaration of Human Rights – articles 20.1 and 23.4
- International Covenant on Economic, Social and Cultural Rights – article 8.1(a)
- International Covenant on Civil and Political Rights – article 22.1
- Beijing Platform for Action – article 178(h)

Healthy and safe working conditions

ILO instruments

- Night Work (Women) Convention, 1919 (No. 4) and ILO Night Work (Women) Convention (Revised), 1934 (No. 41) – article 3
- Night Work of Women (Agriculture) Recommendation, 1921 (No. 13)
- Lead Poisoning (Women and Children) Recommendation, 1919 (No. 4) – paragraphs 1 and 2
- White Lead (Painting) Convention, 1921 (No. 13) – article 3.1
- Underground Work (Women) Convention, 1935 (No. 45) – article 2
- Night Work (Women) Convention (Revised), 1948 (No. 89) – article 3
- Protocol of 1990 to the Night Work (Women) Convention (Revised), 1948 (No. 89) – articles 1.1(1)(c)(ii) and 2.1 and 2.2
- Maternity Protection Recommendation, 1952 (No. 95) – paragraph 5
- Welfare Facilities Recommendation, 1956 (No. 102) – paragraphs 16(1), 19(1) and 34

- Plantations Convention, 1958 (No. 110) – articles 47 and 49
- Discrimination (Employment and Occupation) Recommendation, 1958 (No. 111) – paragraph 2(b)(vi)
- Radiation Protection Recommendation, 1960 (No. 114) – paragraph 16
- Reduction of Hours of Work Recommendation, 1962 (No. 116) – paragraph 18
- Social Policy (Basic Aims and Standards) Convention, 1962 (No. 117) – article 14.1(f) and 14.4
- Maximum Weight Convention, 1967 (No. 127) – article 7
- Maximum Weight Recommendation, 1967 (No. 128) – paragraphs 15–17
- Benzene Convention, 1971 (No. 136) – article 19
- Benzene Recommendation, 1971 (No. 144) – paragraph 19
- Night Work Recommendation, 1990 (No. 178) – paragraphs 10–12 and 13(a) and (b)
- Maternity Protection Convention, 2000 (No. 183) – articles 3, 4.4, 5 and 9
- Maternity Protection Recommendation, 2000 (No. 191) – paragraphs 6–9

Other international instruments

- Convention on the Elimination of All Forms of Discrimination against Women – article 11.1(f)
- International Covenant on Economic, Social and Cultural Rights – article 7(b)

Maternity

ILO instruments

- Declararation of Philadelphia Concerning the Aims and Purpose of the International Labour Organization – article III(h)
- Maternity Protection Convention, 2000 (No. 183) – articles 3–10
- Maternity Protection Recommendation, 2000 (No. 191) – paragraphs 1–10
- Maternity Protection Convention, 1919 (No. 3) – articles 3 and 4
- Maternity Protection (Agriculture) Recommendation, 1921 (No. 12)
- Lead Poisoning (Women and Children) Recommendation, 1919 (No. 4) – paragraph 1
- Protocol of 1990 to the Night Work (Women) Convention (Revised), 1948 (No. 89) – article 2
- Social Security (Minimum Standards) Convention, 1952 (No. 102) – articles 8, 10.1(b), 46–47, 49–50 and 52
- Maternity Protection Convention (Revised), 1952 (No. 103) – articles 3–6
- Maternity Protection Recommendation, 1952 (No. 95) – paragraphs 1(1), 2(1), 3(1), 4(1) and 5

- Plantations Convention, 1958 (No. 110) – articles 47, 48(1) and (2), 49 and 50
- Radiation Protection Recommendation, 1960 (No. 114) – paragraph 16
- Reduction of Hours of Work Recommendation, 1962 (No. 116) – paragraph 18
- Social Policy (Basic Aims and Standards) Convention, 1962 (No. 117) – article 14.4
- Maximum Weight Recommendation, 1967 (No. 128) – paragraph 18
- Benzene Convention, 1971 (No. 136) – article 11.1
- Benzene Recommendation, 1971 (No. 144) – paragraph 19
- Termination of Employment Convention, 1982 (No. 158) – article 5(d) and (e)
- Night Work Convention, 1990 (No. 171) – articles 3.1 and 7
- Night Work Recommendation, 1990 (No. 178) – paragraph 19
- Chemicals Recommendation, 1990 (No. 177) – paragraph 25(4)
- Part-Time Work Recommendation, 1994 (No. 182) – paragraphs 13 and 20

Other international instruments

- Universal Declaration of Human Rights – article 25.2
- Convention on the Elimination of all Forms of Discrimination against Women – Preamble and articles 4.2, 11.2 and 12.2
- International Covenant on Economic, Social and Cultural Rights – article 10.2
- Beijing Platform for Action – paragraph 178(d)

Appropriate measures to allow women workers with family responsibilities to reconcile these responsibilities and their professional obligations

ILO instruments

- Workers with Family Responsibilities Convention, 1981 (No. 156) – articles 3–5 and 7
- Workers with Family Responsibilities Recommendation, 1981 (No. 165) – paragraphs 6, 7, 9, 15, 17, 25 and 32
- Protocol of 1990 to the Night Work (Women) Convention (Revised), 1948 (No. 89) – article 2.3(b)
- Protection of Wages Convention, 1949 (No. 95) – article 10.2
- Social Security (Minimum Standards) Convention, 1952 (No. 102) – articles 39–40 and 42
- Maternity Protection Convention (Revised), 1952 (No. 103) – article 4.2
- Maternity Protection Recommendation, 1952 (No. 95) – paragraph 3(2)
- Plantations Convention, 1958 (No. 110) – article 48(2)
- Social Policy (Basic Aims and Standards) Convention, 1962 (No. 117) – article 5

- Paid Educational Leave Convention, 1974 (No. 140) – article 9(a)
- Human Resources Development Recommendation, 1975 (No. 150) – paragraph 54(2)(e)
- Termination of Employment Convention, 1982 (No. 158) – article 5(d)
- Employment Policy (Supplementary Provisions) Recommendation, 1984 (No. 169) – paragraph 14
- Night Work Convention, 1990 (No. 171) – article 3.1
- Night Work Recommendation, 1990 (No. 178) – paragraph 20
- Part-Time Work Recommendation, 1994 (No. 182) – paragraph 20
- Maternity Protection Convention, 2000 (No. 183) – article 10
- Maternity Protection Recommendation, 2000 (No. 191) – paragraph 10

Other international instruments

- Universal Declaration of Human Rights – article 16.3
- International Covenant on Economic, Social and Cultural Rights – article 10.1
- International Covenant on Civil and Political Rights – article 23.1
- Convention on the Elimination of All Forms of Discrimination against Women – articles 10(h) and 11.2(c)
- Beijing Platform for Action – paragraphs 179(c) and 180(a)
- Convention on the Rights of the Child – article 18.3

Part-time workers

ILO instruments

- Workers with Family Responsibilities Recommendation, 1981 (No. 165) – paragraph 21(1) and (2)
- Employment Promotion and Protection against Unemployment Convention, 1988 (No. 168) – article 25.1
- Part-Time Work Convention, 1994 (No. 175) – articles 4–7
- Part-Time Work Recommendation, 1994 (No. 182) – paragraphs 7(2), 10–11 and 13–15

Home workers

ILO instruments

- Workers with Family Responsibilities Recommendation, 1981 (No. 165) – paragraph 21(1)
- Home Work Convention, 1996 (No. 177) – articles 3 and 4
- Home Work Recommendation, 1996 (No. 184) – paragraphs 11, 13, 15 and 24–27

A DEFINITION OF SEXUAL HARASSMENT   Appendix XIII

(taken from *Action against sexual harassment at work in Asia and the Pacific*, ILO, 2001)

While perceptions on what constitutes sexual harassment vary among and within societies, depending on whether individuals are born and socialized as men or women in a specific socio-economic class in a society and on their position in the work hierarchy, universal consensus exists on the key characteristics of definitions on sexual harassment.

Generally speaking, definitions used in laws, codes, policies, court decisions and collective agreements throughout the world may differ in details but they contain the following key elements:

- conduct of a sexual nature and other conduct based on sex affecting the dignity of women and men, which is unwelcome, unreasonable and offensive to the recipient;
- a person's rejection of, or submission to, such conduct is used explicitly or implicitly as a basis for a decision which affects that person's job;
- conduct that creates an intimidating, hostile or humiliating work environment for the recipient.

EU EQUALITY OF OPPORTUNITY AND TREATMENT IN RESPECT OF EMPLOYMENT AND OCCUPATION: A SUMMARY

The Council of the EU has, since 1975, approved a group of Directives aimed at equal treatment and equal opportunities between men and women. This is applicable to different professions within the EU.

In 1975, **Council Directive 75/117/EC of 10 February 1975 on the approximation of the laws of the Member States relating to the application of the principle of equal pay for men and women** was adopted. This Directive defines the "principle of equal pay" for the same work or for work to which equal value is attributed, "the elimination of discrimination on grounds of sex with regard to all aspects and conditions of remuneration". Article 1 adds that "where a job classification system is used for determining pay, it must be based on the same criteria for both men and women and so drawn up as to exclude any discrimination on grounds of sex".

This first Directive was followed in 1976 by **Council Directive 76/207/EEC of 9 February 1976 on the implementation of the principle of equal treatment for men and women as regards access to employment, vocational training and promotion, and working conditions**. The purpose of the Directive was "to put into effect in the Member States the principle of equal treatment for men and women as regards access to employment, including promotion, and to vocational training and as regards working conditions and [...] on the conditions referred to social security". Furthermore, the Directive adds that the principle of equal treatment "shall mean that there shall be no discrimination whatsoever on grounds of sex either directly or indirectly by reference in particular to marital or family status" nor "discrimination on grounds of sex in the conditions, including selection criteria for access to all jobs or posts". Based on the Directive, the principle should allow equal treatment with respect to access to training, working conditions and the conditions governing dismissal.

In 1978, **Council Directive 79/7/EEC of 19 December 1978 on the progressive implementation of the principle of equal treatment for men and women in matters of social security** was adopted. The objective was to implement progressively the principle of equal treatment in the field of social security and other elements of social protection.

The following Directive related to equal opportunities was adopted by the Council only in 1986: **Council Directive 86/378/EEC of 24 July 1986 on the implementation of the principle of equal treatment for men and women in occupational social security schemes.** The objective was to implement "in occupational social security schemes, the principle of equal treatment for men and women".

In the same year, the Council adopted **Directive 86/613/EEC of 11 December on the application of the principle of equal treatment between men and women engaged in an activity, including agriculture, in a self-employed capacity, and on the protection of self-employed women during pregnancy and motherhood.** The main objective was to ensure equal treatment between self-employed male and female workers.

It took a further six years for another Directive affecting the employment of women to be adopted. In 1992, the Council adopted **Directive 92/85/EEC of 19 October on the introduction of measures to encourage improvements in the safety and health at work of pregnant workers and workers who have recently given birth or are breastfeeding.** The purpose of the Directive, which was the tenth individual Directive within the meaning of Article 16(1) of Directive 89/391/EEC,[1] "is to implement measures to encourage improvements in the safety and health at work of pregnant workers and workers who have recently given birth or who are breastfeeding" (Article 1(1)).

In 1997, **Council Directive 97/80/EC of 15 December on the burden of proof in cases of discrimination based on sex** was adopted. The aim of the Directive "is to ensure that the measures taken by Member States to implement the principle of equal treatment are made more effective, in order to enable all persons who consider themselves wronged because the principle of equal treatment has not been applied to them to have their rights asserted by judicial process after possible recourse to other competent bodies".

Finally, the most recent and relevant Directive was adopted in 2000: **Council Directive 2000/78/EC of 27 November establishing a general framework for equal treatment in employment and occupation.** The purpose of this Directive "is to lay down a general framework for combating discrimination on the grounds of religion or belief, disability, age or sexual orientation as regards employment and occupation, with a view to putting into effect in the Member States the principle of equal treatment" – Article 1. Among the most important articles of this Directive are the following:

Article 10 – Burden of proof: "1. Member States shall take such measures as are necessary, in accordance with their national judicial systems, to ensure that, when persons who consider themselves wronged because the principle of equal treatment has not been applied to them establish, before a court or other competent authority, facts from which it may be presumed that there has been direct or indirect discrimination, it shall be for the respondent to prove that there has been no breach of the principle of equal treatment."

---

[1] Council Directive 89/391/EEC of 12 June 1989 on the introduction of measures to encourage improvements in the safety and health of workers at work.

Article 11 – Victimization: "Member States shall introduce into their national legal systems such measures as are necessary to protect employees against dismissal or other adverse treatment by the employer as a reaction to a complaint within the undertaking or to any legal proceedings aimed at enforcing compliance with the principle of equal treatment."

Apart from the above-mentioned Directives, it is also worth highlighting **Council Directive 96/34/EC of 3 June 1996 on the framework agreement on parental leave** concluded by the Union of Industrial and Employers' Confederations of Europe (UNICE), the European Centre of Enterprises with Public Participation and of Enterprises of General Economic Interest (CEEP) and the European Trade Union Confederation (ETUC). The framework agreement on parental leave brought into the effect by the Directive was concluded on 14 December 1995 between the general cross-industry organizations UNICE, CEEP and the ETUC. It was enacted under the Social Policy Agreement (SPA) protocol to the EC treaty. Both male and female workers are given a non-transferable individual right to parental leave "on the grounds of the birth or adoption of a child to enable them to take care of that child, for at least three months, until a given age up to 8 years to be defined by Member States and/or management and labour".

Apart from the compulsory Directives mentioned above, there are several other Commission Decisions[2] and a Council Regulation[3] that regulate the work of women.

Council Regulation No. 2836/98 of 22 December 1998 on integrating gender in development cooperation aims "to systematically integrate gender mainstreaming as a guiding principle into the conception, design, implementation and evaluation of all development interventions and strategies". The Regulation also states that gender issues are taken to include "the different and interrelated roles, responsibilities and opportunities of women and men relative to development, which are culturally specific and socially constructed, and can change over time, inter alia, as a result of policy interventions" – Article 1(3).

The following Commission Decisions and Recommendations relate specifically to gender issues and in particular to the employment of women:

- Commission Decision 82/43/EEC of 9 December 1981 relating to the setting-up of an Advisory Committee on Equal Opportunities for Women and Men as amended by the Commission Decision 95/420/EC of 19 July 1995;

- Commission Recommendation 87/567/EEC of 24 November 1987 on vocational training for women;

- Commission Recommendation 92/131/EEC of 27 November 1991 on the protection of the dignity of women and men at work. This Recommendation aims to "promote greater awareness of the problem of sexual harassment at work and its consequences; draw attention to the Commission Code of Conduct *Protecting the dignity of women and men at work: A code of practice on measures to combat sexual harassment* and recommends the application of this code to Member States";

---

[2] Decisions are Community laws, issued by either the Council of the EU or the European Commission, which are directly binding on those to whom the Decisions are addressed (governments, companies, or individuals). They are usually directed at a specific Member State or organization or individuals and require specific action, which is binding on those to whom the decision is addressed.

[3] Council Regulations are binding in their entirety.

- 95/593/EC: Council Decision of 22 December 1995 on a medium-term Community Action Programme on equal opportunities for men and women (1996–2000);
- 2000/228/EC: Council Decision of 13 March 2000 on guidelines for Member States' employment policies for the year 2000;
- 00/407/EC: Commission Decision of 19 June 2000 relating to gender balance within the communities and expert groups established by it (notified under document number C(2000) 1600);
- 2000/750/EC: Council Decision of 27 November 2000, establishing a Community Action Programme to combat discrimination (2001–06);
- 2001/51/EC: Council Decision of 20 December 2000, establishing a Programme relating to the Community framework strategy on gender equality (2001–05);
- 2001/63/EC: Council Decision of 19 January 2001 on guidelines for Member States' employment policies for the year 2001.

Within the EU's legislative measures, it is also worth referring to Communication 2000 (COM(99) 441) on *Equal opportunities for women and men in the fourth pillar of the employment guidelines for 2000*.

Specifically for maritime transport, the Commission of the European Communities in its *Communication from the Commission to the Council and the European Parliament on the training and recruitment of seafarers*[4] proposes that the social partners "make every effort to promote and facilitate women's access to the seafaring professions, especially those which may be more attractive to women".[5] Furthermore, the Commission recognizes that awareness campaigns might be a useful tool. It adds that the "social partners should also tackle the existing unacceptable problems of discrimination and prejudice encountered by many women employed aboard EU ships".[6] Finally, the *Communication* states that:

> Measures to promote female employment on board ships would be in line with the IMO plan for the integration of women in the maritime sector and with the Standards of Training, Certification and Watchkeeping (STCW) Recommendation that special consideration be given to securing equal access by men and women in all sectors of the maritime industry, that the role of women in the seafaring profession be highlighted and that their increased participation be promoted in maritime training and at all levels in the maritime industry. All measures to promote female employment on board EU ships and to combat discrimination and prejudice against women would be also in line with the general Community policy of equal treatment for men and women.[7]

The European Commission also recognizes that shipowners can do a lot to make life on board more attractive, both in the living and working conditions as well as through the introduction of modern information technologies.[8]

---

[4] COM(2001) 188 final of 6 April 2001.
[5] ibid., p. 13.
[6] ibid.
[7] ibid., p. 14.
[8] ibid.

GOVERNMENT POLICY RELEVANT TO WOMEN SEAFARERS IN CHINA: A SUMMARY[1]

The Chinese Government has no tailor-made policy on women seafarers. However, women seafarers come under the protection of a considerable number of policies, regulations and laws introduced since 1986 with the objective of protecting women workers across industries and sectors. These policies, regulations and laws include the following:

- *Temporary regulations on the health and protection of women employees (draft)*, 30 May 1993, issued jointly by the Ministry of Public Health, the Ministry of Labour and Personnel, the All-China Federation of Trade Unions (ACFTU) and the All-China Women's Federation (ACWF);

- *Regulations on labour protection of women employees*, 21 July 1988, State Council;

- *Notes on issues with regard to women employees' maternity wages and welfare treatment*, Ministry of Labour, 1 September 1990;

- *Stipulation on jobs and occupations where women's employment is forbidden*,[2] Ministry of Labour, 10 October 1990;

- *Law on the protection of women's rights and interests, People's Republic of China*, 5th Session, The 7th People's Congress, April 1992;

- *Regulations on the health and protection of women employees*, issued jointly by the Ministry of Public Health, the Ministry of Labour and Personnel, the ACFTU and the ACWF, November 1993;

- *Labour law (Chapter 7: Special protection for women employees and young people between 16 and 18)*, 5 July 1994, The People's Congress.

Furthermore, the regulation, *Labour protection for women workers in transportation: Implementation procedures*,[3] based on the labour law and issued by the Ministry of

---

[1] The main source of this summary is: L. Dong and J. Shen (eds.), 1999, *Studies of the labour law (new version): Theories of the trade union*, Textbook Series (Zhuhai, Zhuhai Publishing House, ISBN 7-80607-602-6), pp. 136–142.

[2] The occupations in which women are positively protected from participating include certain jobs in mining, forestry, construction and electricity as well as jobs that require the carrying of heavy loads. Shipping or seafaring is not included as being unsuitable for women.

[3] This regulation was referred to by the senior officials of China's Ministry of Transport and the Chinese Seafarers Trade Union during the researcher's interviews with them in Beijing, 5–7 Nov. 2001.

Transport, specifies the protection measures and procedures relevant to women's employment rights, menstruation, pregnancy, maternity and childcare. The following clauses are particularly relevant:

- Clause 4: The company is not allowed to discriminate against women in recruitment – either by refusal or by increasing the recruitment standard – on the grounds of their sex (except those companies that are not allowed to employ women due to the fact that their jobs or occupations are specified by state law or regulation as unsuitable for women).[4]

- Clause 8: [...] It should be arranged that women employed in construction, road maintenance, motor vehicle driving, port loading/unloading and in the hotel/catering sector on board ships should conduct other jobs when they are five months into their pregnancy.[5]

- Clause 9: All women employed in the industry are entitled to 90 days' paid maternity leave. During this period, they are entitled to the same welfare treatment as before.

Clearly, considerable efforts have been made by the Chinese Government to ensure that there are laws and policies for the protection of women workers in the country. In terms of policy-making, China seems to have an impressive record, although the existence of a policy does not necessarily guarantee that the policy will be effectively implemented.

---

[4] See footnote 2.

[5] This clearly indicates the country's policy on pregnancy for women seafarers.

BIBLIOGRAPHY

Belcher, P.; Lane, A.D.; Sampson, H; Thomas, M.; Veiga, J.; Zhao, M. 2001. *Women seafarers; A survey of global employment issues and practices*, SIRC/ILO Survey Report commissioned by the International Labour Organization (Geneva, ILO).

—; Winchester, N. 2002. "Economic Review 2001", in *Flags of Convenience Campaign Report 2001* (London, International Transport Workers' Federation).

Casagrande, S. 1999 "Women at sea: Three ladies among 1,500 men, Germany's female masters", based on the Women at sea exhibition in a museum at Wischafen near Hamburg, in *Lloyd's List*, 17 July, p. 7.

Chamber of Shipping (COS). 1995. *COS Manpower Inquiry 1995* (London).

Chapman, P. 1992. *Trouble on board: The plight of international seafarers* (New York, ILR Press).

Creighton, S.M. 1992. "Women and men in American whaling, 1830–1870", in *International Journal of Maritime History*, Vol. IV, No. 1, June, pp. 195–218.

—; Norling, L. 1996. *Iron men, wooden women: Gender and seafaring in the Atlantic world, 1700–1920* (Baltimore, Johns Hopkins University Press).

Dana, R.H. 1925. *Two years before the mast* (London, J.M. Dent).

Dong, L.; Shen, J. (eds.). 1999. *Studies of the labour law (new version): Theories of the trade union*, Textbook Series (Zhuhai, Zhuhai Publishing House).

Drummond, J.C. 1999. *The remarkable life of Victoria Drummond, marine engineer* (London, Institute of Marine Engineers).

Dugaw, D. 1992. "Rambling female sailors: The rise and fall of the seafaring heroine", in *International Journal of Maritime History*, Vol. IV, No. 1, June, pp. 179–194.

Effective Change Pty Ltd. 1995. *Women at sea: Policy discussion paper* (London).

European Commission. 2001. *Communication from the Commission to the Council and the European Parliament on the training and recruitment of seafarers* (Brussels, COM(2001) 188).

Fairplay. "India encourages women seafarers", 31 Oct., 2002, p. 7.

—. "Déjà Vu", 9 Jan., 2003, p. 52.

Federal Ministry of Employment and Labour. 1997. *Belgian pool of seafarers* (Brussels).

Fournier, C.A. 1993. "Undercurrents: The experiences of New England maritime women, 1790–1912", unpublished dissertation, University of Hawaii.

Higher Education Statistics Agency (HESA). 1997. *Resources of Higher Education Institutions 1995/1996* (Cheltenham).

Institute of Employment Research (IER). 1995. *BIMCO/ISF Manpower Survey* (London, BIMCO/ISF).

—. 2000. *BIMCO/ISF 2000 Manpower Update* (London, BIMCO/ISF).

Institute of Shipping Economics and Logistics (ISL). 1998. *Shipping Statistics Year Book 1998* (Bremen).

International Labour Office (ILO). 2001. *The impact on seafarers' living and working conditions of changes in the structure of the shipping industry*, Report for discussion at the 29th Session of the Joint Maritime Committee (Geneva).

International Maritime Organization (IMO). 1988. *Strategy for the integration of women in the maritime sector* (London).

—. 1992. *1992–1996 Medium-term plan for the integration of women in the maritime sector* (London).

—. 1997. *Action programme for equal opportunities and advancement of women in the maritime sector 1997–2001* (London).

—. 2001. *IMO/Norway cooperation programme impact assessment exercise 2000: Review of the WID sub-programme*, IMO Internal Document, Annex XIV, Feb. (Oslo, IMO).

International Shipping Federation (ISF). 2001. *Guidelines on good employment practice (Discrimination and Abuse)* (London, Maritime International Secretariat Services Ltd.).

International Transport Workers' Federation (ITF). 1996. "Who are ITF women?: Survey results", in *ITF Women*, No. 1, p. 6.

—. 2000. "The ITF/IMEC Model TCC Agreeement" (attached as Appendix I), in *ITF/IMEC Joint-Negotiating Forum*, 6 July.

Keitsch, C. 1997. *Women at sea* (Flensburg, Museum of Flensburg).

La marine merchande en guerre, booklet in Professor A.D. Lane's (director of the SIRC) private library (publisher and publication date missing).

Lane, A. D. 1986. *Grey dawn breaking: British merchant seafarers in the late 20th century* (Manchester, Manchester University Press).

—. 1990. *The merchant seamen's war* (Manchester, Manchester University Press).

—; et al. 2002. *Crewing the international merchant fleet* (London, Lloyd's Register, Fairplay).

Maritime and Coastguard Agency (MCA). 1997a. "New and expectant mothers: Health and safety", in *MCA Marine Guidance Note*, MGN 112 (M+F), MC11/4/02, MS 122/6/47 (Southampton).

—. 1997b. "New and expectant mothers: Merchant shipping and fishing vessels", Health and Safety at Work Regulations, in *MCA Marine Guidance Note*, MGN 112 (M+F) (Southampton).

—. 2000. *Business plan 2000–2001 and forward look* (Southampton).

National Union of Maritime and Aviation Shipping Transport Officers (NUMAST). 1981. "Barriers against women at sea are crumbling in most countries", in *NUMAST Telegraph*, Jan., p. 16.

—. 1997. "Council's report to the biennial general meeting", in *NUMAST Telegraph*, May, p. 5.

Peisley, T. 1996. *The world cruise ship industry to 2000, Research report* (London, Travel & Tourism Intelligence).

Rodriguez-Martos, R. 1995. "The merchant vessel as a total institution", PhD thesis submitted to the Universitat Politècnica de Catalunya, Barcelona.

Stanley, J. 1987. *Women at sea* (published by the author, c/o 23, Nazeby Avenue, Crosby, Liverpool).

Stark, S.J. 1998. *Female tars: Women aboard ship in the age of sail* (London, Pimlico).

Tao, H.; Zhou, R. 2000. "A historical breakthrough at Shanghai Maritime University: 18 female students enrol in its navigation department", in *Wenhui Daily*, 8 Aug., p. 1.

Tutt, N. 2001. "European drive to reverse fall in seafarers", in *Lloyd's List*, 20 Apr., p. 3.

Wild, G.B. 1999. "Human resources in the cruise industry", in *Cruise & Ferry '99*, Paper Collection, p. 13.

Zhao, M. 1998. *Women seafarers in the EC: A preliminary report based on German and United Kingdom case studies* (Cardiff University, Cardiff, SIRC).

—. 1999. "Women seafarers", Working Paper delivered to the ILO, Geneva (Cardiff University, Cardiff, SIRC).

—. 2001. "The role of female crew members on board cruise ships", in *Proceedings of the Cruise & Ferry Conference 2001*, 3–5 March, London.

INDEX

Note: Page numbers in **bold** refer to major text sections, those in *italic* to figures.